THE BACKGROUND OF MICROSOFT TEAM

"Unveiling the Dynamic Tapestry: Tracing the Evolution and Innovations that Shaped Microsoft Teams for Beginners"

ERNEST TWAIN

Copyright© 2024 by **ERNEST TWAIN**

All right reserved

No part of this book be reproduced in any form, stored in a retrieval system or transmitted in any manner electronic, mechanical, photocopying, recording, or otherwise, without the prior written permission of the publisher, except is permitted United States copyright law and fair use.

Discaimer and Term of Use

The author and publisher of this book, along with the accompanying materials, have made every effort to ensure its accuracy, applicability, fitness and completeness. However, they do not provide any representations or warranties regarding the contents of this book. The information contained herein is intenced solely for informational purposes. Consequently, if you choose to implement the concepts presented in this book, you do so at your discretion and assume full responsibility for your actions

Printed in the United States of America.

TABLE OF CONTENTS

TABLE OF CONTENTS iii

INTRODUCTION 1

CHAPTER 1 3

GETTING STARTED WITH MICROSOFT TEAMS 3

GETTING UP AND RUNNING WITH MICROSOFT TEAMS 3

   GETTING STARTED WITH TEAMS APP 3
      Downloading and Installing Teams for PC: 3
      Similarities and Differences between Teams Application for PC and Teams Web App 4

   GETTING TEAMS FOR FREE 5

   GETTING TEAMS THROUGH OFFICE 365 6
      Teams and Channels 7

   WRAPPING YOUR HEAD AROUND MICROSOFT TEAMS 8

   GETTING FAMILIAR WITH TEAMS TERMINOLOGY 10

   BELOW ARE TWO TYPES OF MICROSOFT TEAMS 11

CHAPTER 2 13

NAVIGATING MICROSOFT TEAMS 13

   DOWNLOADING, INSTALLING AND OPENING TEAMS 13

   TAKING QUICK SPIN AROUND THE TEAMS ACTIVITY 18

   CHAT 19

   TEAMS 21

   CALENDER 22
      How Microsoft Teams Calendars Work 23
      How to Create a Microsoft Teams Shared Calendar Event 23

   CALLS 25

   FILES 25
      Your files library 26

   USING TEAMS ACROSS MANY DEVICE AND PLATFORM 27

CHAPTER 3 28

STARTING YOUR FIRST TEAM AND MANAGING YOUR SETTINGS **28**
    CREATING A NEW TEAMS *28*
    INVITING PEOPLE TO YOUR TEAM *30*
    MANAGING YOUR TEAM SETTINGS *31*
    MANAGING YOUR USER SETTINGS *34*
        The profile drop-down menu. 34

CHAPTER 4 .... **40**

STAYING CONNECTED TO OTHERS WITH CHANNELS AND CHAT **40**
    CHATTING IN TEAMS *40*
    SENDING MESSAGES IN CHANNELS *41*
    CREATING A NEW CHANNEL *43*
    CONFIGURING A CHANNEL *46*
    MOVING FROM A CHANNEL TO A CHAT *48*
    STARTING A PRIVATE CHAT *50*
    ADDING MULTIPLE PEOPLE TO A CHAT *51*
    GIVING A CHAT A TITLE *52*
    PINNING A CHAT TO THE TOP OF THE LIST *53*
    SENDING MORE THAN TEXT WHEN CHATTING *54*
    ADDING EMOJIS, GIFs, AND STICKERS *54*

CHAPTER 5 .... **59**

EXTENDING TEAMS WITH APPS **59**
    DISCOVERING APPS ALREADY INSTALLED *59*
        THE FILE TAB 59
        THE WIKI TAB 60
        Chat from Wiki tab 61
    BROWSING AND ADDING APPS *62*
        ADD APP TO TEAMS 62
    EXPLORING POPULAR APPS *62*
    POPULAR APPS FROM MICROSOFT *65*
    POPULAR APPS FROM THIRD-PARTY COMPANIES *68*

  Connectors 68
  Bots 70
  Tabs 71
 SETTING PERMISSIONS FOR APPS 72
  App Permission Policies 72
  Create a custom app permission policy 73
 GETTING CHATTY WITH BOTS 74
  Microsoft Teams bots 75

CHAPTER 6 79

UNSHACKLING YOURSELF WITH TEAMS ON MOBILE 79

 INSTALLING THE TEAMS MOBILE APPS 79
  Installing on iOS 79
  Installing on Android 80
  Installing the Teams app from the Google Play Store. 81
  Find your way around the Teams mobile app 82
  Tapping your way through Teams 84
  Interacting with messages 84
  Reacting to a message using Teams on a desktop or laptop computer. 85
  Reacting to a message using Teams on a phone or tablet 86
 GETTING USED TO NAVIGATION 86

CONCLUSION 89

INTRODUCTION

Microsoft Teams stands as an indispensable tool within your group's arsenal, serving as a dynamic hub for seamless collaboration and communication. It functions as a comprehensive workstation, offering a spectrum of features including real-time messaging, video conferencing capabilities, file sharing functionalities, and even the subtle touch of emoticons for added expression. All these elements converge within a unified platform, easily accessible to all members. At its core, Microsoft Teams is a multifaceted communication and collaboration platform, weaving together chat functionalities, video conferencing capabilities, file storage solutions, and seamless integration with various applications. It seamlessly integrates into the Microsoft Office 365 suite, ensuring accessibility across web browsers, desktop applications, and mobile devices. The platform serves as a catalyst for effective communication and collaboration among team members, addressing various challenges encountered in online intercommunication. From fostering real-time discussions to streamlining file management processes, Microsoft Teams offers a plethora of benefits that streamline workflow and enhance productivity.

Here are some key reasons why Microsoft Teams has become an integral part of our workflow:

1. **Multifaceted Communication:** Users can engage in diverse forms of communication, including text-based chats, audio calls, video meetings, and file sharing functionalities, enabling seamless interaction among team members.

2. **Private Chat Functionality:** The platform facilitates private chats, fostering an environment conducive to knowledge sharing and collaborative problem-solving.

3. **Centralized File Storage:** Microsoft Teams serves as a centralized repository for storing files, documents, and various resources, ensuring easy access and streamlined collaboration.

4. **Application Integration:** Through its robust integration capabilities, Microsoft Teams allows users to seamlessly incorporate their favorite productivity apps, such as Planner, Trello, GitHub, and more, enhancing workflow efficiency and facilitating project management.

In summary, Microsoft Teams embodies more than just a messaging app; it serves as a comprehensive ecosystem tailored to meet the evolving needs of modern teams, fostering seamless collaboration, streamlined communication, and enhanced productivity.

CHAPTER 1

GETTING STARTED WITH MICROSOFT TEAMS

GETTING UP AND RUNNING WITH MICROSOFT TEAMS

GETTING STARTED WITH TEAMS APP

It seems like you want me to explain how to download and install the Teams app for PC or laptop, as well as highlight the similarities and differences between the Teams application for PC and the Teams web app. Let's break it down:

Downloading and Installing Teams for PC:

1. **Visit the Microsoft Teams Website**: Go to the official Microsoft Teams website (https://www.microsoft.com/en-us/microsoft-365/microsoft-teams/download-app) to download the application.

2. **Choose your Platform**: Microsoft Teams is available for Windows, macOS, iOS, and Android. Make sure to select the version compatible with your PC's operating system.

3. **Download the Installer**: Click on the "Download Teams" button. This will initiate the download of the Teams installer file.

4. **Run the Installer**: Once the download is complete, locate the installer file in your Downloads folder or wherever you chose to save it. Double-click on the installer file to run it.

5. **Follow Installation Prompts**: The installer will guide you through the installation process. Follow the on-screen instructions, such as agreeing to the license terms and choosing the installation location.

6. **Launch Teams**: After installation is complete, you can launch the Teams application from your desktop or start menu.

Similarities and Differences between Teams Application for PC and Teams Web App

Similarities:

- **User Interface**: Both the Teams application for PC and the Teams web app have a similar user interface. They provide access to the same features and functionalities.

- **Core Features**: Both versions allow users to chat, make audio and video calls, join meetings, collaborate on documents, and access channels and teams.

- **Integration**: They both integrate seamlessly with other Microsoft 365 applications like Outlook, OneDrive, and SharePoint.

Differences:

- **Performance**: The Teams application for PC may offer better performance compared to the web app, as it is optimized to run natively on your computer.

- **Offline Access**: The Teams application for PC allows users to access their messages, files, and content even when they are offline, whereas the web app requires an internet connection.

- **Notifications**: The PC application may provide more customizable notification options compared to the web app, allowing users to stay updated on activity even when they're not actively using Teams.

- **Access to System Resources**: The PC application may have access to more system resources, enabling smoother performance and faster response times compared to running Teams in a web browser.

In summary, while both the Teams application for PC and the Teams web app offer similar features and functionalities, the PC application may provide a better user experience in terms of performance, offline access, and system integration.

The PC application has a few more features such as the ability to make your background unclear in a team meeting. The installed Teams app is the most reliable method of using Teams, but don't wait to use the net client instead when it's appropriate - it's very good.

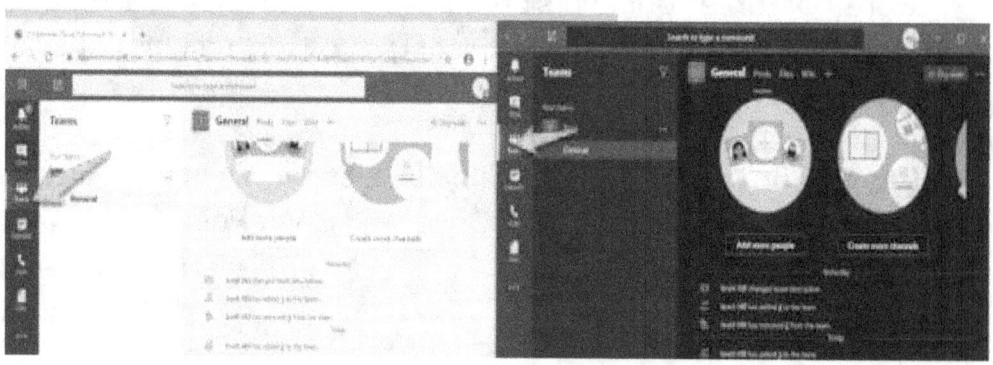

GETTING TEAMS FOR FREE

Teams offer several benefits, however, for the sake of competitors like Slack, Microsoft came up with a free edition of teams in 2018. "With the complimentary version of Microsoft Teams, users gain access to a plethora of communication and collaboration features. Enjoy unlimited chats, audio calls, and video calls, facilitating seamless interaction within your team. Additionally, you'll have the convenience of 10GB of file storage dedicated to your team's projects, complemented by an additional 2GB of personal storage space allotted to each team member.

Microsoft Teams boasts seamless integration with all online Office applications, streamlining productivity by enabling easy access to essential tools. Furthermore, it offers compatibility with over 140 business applications, ensuring versatility and adaptability to diverse workplace needs. Expanding your network is effortless with Microsoft Teams, as you can effortlessly link up to 250 contacts within your organization. This facilitates efficient communication and collaboration across departments and teams, fostering a cohesive work environment.

It's important to note that the free version of Microsoft Teams is exclusively available to individuals without an active paid commercial Office 365 subscription. Subscribers of Office 365 attempting to access Teams are directed to their managed account corresponding to their existing plan. However, for those without a Teams license as part of their Office 365 subscription, there's the option to register for a complimentary one-year trial, allowing them to experience the full benefits of Teams' collaborative features." Sometimes you may have an office 365 subscription and you will like to use teams for free, you can register with a different email address. If the address has been used for Microsoft Account, Teams will set it up sequentially.

GETTING TEAMS THROUGH OFFICE 365

Before getting started it's necessary to understand how Teams fits into the larger Office 365 picture, as creating Teams has broad implications. Every Team created, will create a matching plan automatically, SharePoint Team Site, Office 365 Group, and shared OneNote. While this brings several countless profits, such as shared documents and unified team information, it can cause some governance and admin headaches. Luckily, the admin side of Teams allows this to be managed as we'll cover below. Once your organization has entree to Teams, you can: download the desktop application, access Teams through your browser.

Teams and Channels

To initiate collaborative teamwork, the first step is assembling your team. The process of setting up Teams is straightforward, requiring just a few clicks. All you need is a Team name and a brief description. This basic information allows for the addition of team members. However, it's essential to exercise some caution during this setup phase, as each new Team generates corresponding assets within Office 365, including a Group, OneNote, SharePoint site, and Plan.

Each Team is further organized into subdivisions known as Channels, with a default General Channel automatically created. Within a Team, you can establish multiple Channels to facilitate focused discussions and tasks. For instance, if you're managing a 'Marketing' Team, you might create Channels such as 'Social Media,' 'Product Launch,' and 'Blogs.' Alternatively, if your organization is the Team, Channels can be tailored to specific sectors or projects, allowing for flexibility in alignment with your organization's workflow. Notifications and activity within Channels are signaled by bolding the respective Channel name, ensuring that team members stay updated on relevant discussions and developments.

WRAPPING YOUR HEAD AROUND MICROSOFT TEAMS

Absolutely! Microsoft Teams is a collaboration platform developed by Microsoft as part of the Office 365 suite of productivity tools. It's designed to facilitate communication and collaboration within teams and organizations, offering a wide range of features to streamline workflows and enhance productivity. Let's break down some of its key features and purposes:

1. **Chat-based Communication**: At its core, Teams provides chat-based communication, allowing team members to send instant messages, share files, and collaborate in real-time. Users can create different chat channels for specific topics, projects, or departments, enabling focused discussions and easy information sharing.

2. **Integration with Office 365**: One of the major advantages of Teams is its seamless integration with other Office 365 applications such as Word, Excel, PowerPoint, and OneNote. Users can edit and collaborate on documents directly within Teams, eliminating the need to switch between different applications.

3. **Meetings and Video Conferencing**: Teams offers robust meeting and video conferencing capabilities, enabling teams to conduct virtual meetings with audio, video, and screen sharing functionalities. It supports scheduled meetings, ad-hoc calls, and even large-scale live events, making it suitable for various collaboration scenarios.

4. **File Sharing and Collaboration**: Teams allows users to share files within chat channels, making it easy to collaborate on documents,

presentations, spreadsheets, and other files. Files are stored securely in SharePoint or OneDrive, ensuring accessibility and version control.

5. **Team Collaboration Spaces**: Teams provides dedicated spaces for teams to collaborate, organize tasks, and manage projects. These spaces include features such as tabs for apps and tools, customizable channels, and integration with third-party services like Trello and Asana.

6. **Security and Compliance**: Microsoft Teams prioritizes security and compliance, offering features such as data encryption, multi-factor authentication, and compliance with industry regulations such as GDPR and HIPAA. This ensures that sensitive information is protected and that Teams can be used in regulated industries.

Now, as for tips on how to make the most of Microsoft Teams to boost your team's efficiency:

1. **Customize Your Workspace**: Tailor Teams to suit your team's specific needs by creating custom channels, adding tabs for frequently used apps and tools, and adjusting notification settings to minimize distractions.

2. **Use @Mentions and Tags**: Utilize @mentions to direct messages to specific team members or channels, ensuring that important communications are seen promptly. You can also use tags to group team members based on roles, departments, or projects for easier communication.

3. **Schedule and Conduct Efficient Meetings**: Use the built-in calendar feature to schedule meetings directly within Teams, and leverage features like screen sharing, meeting notes, and recording to facilitate productive discussions and collaborations during meetings.

4. **Integrate Third-Party Apps and Services**: Take advantage of Teams' integration capabilities by connecting third-party apps and services that your team uses regularly, such as project management tools, customer relationship management (CRM) systems, or analytics platforms.

5. **Encourage Collaboration and Feedback**: Foster a culture of collaboration and feedback within your team by actively encouraging participation in chat channels, sharing updates and insights, and soliciting input on projects and initiatives.

6. **Stay Organized with Channels and Tabs**: Organize your team's conversations and resources by creating dedicated channels for different topics or projects, and utilize tabs to add relevant apps, documents, or websites for easy access.

By leveraging these features and implementing these tips, you can maximize the efficiency and effectiveness of your team's collaboration efforts using Microsoft Teams.

GETTING FAMILIAR WITH TEAMS TERMINOLOGY

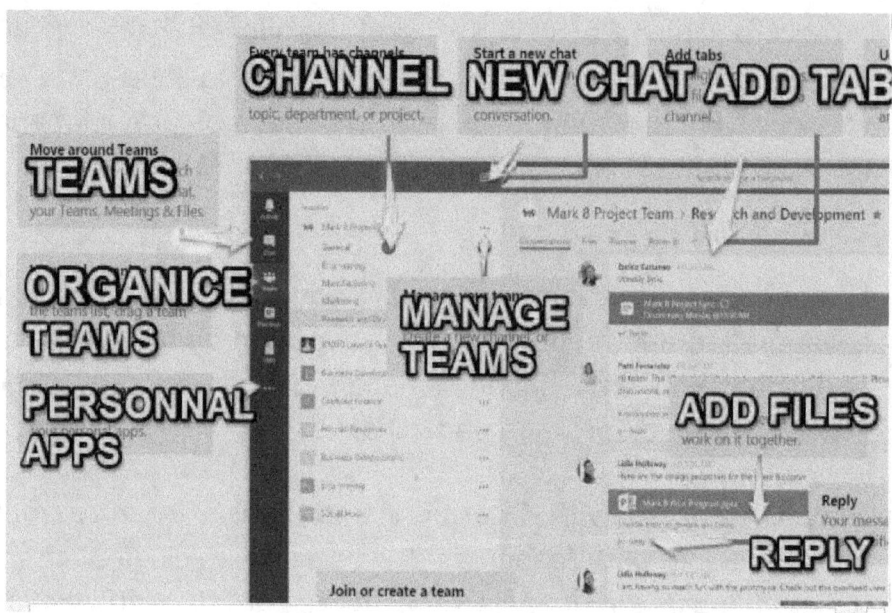

A team is a collection of people working towards a common goal or employed to deliver a task. Teams are made on Microsoft 365 Groups – the introductory membership service that energies all teamwork across Office 365.

A team includes the content and tools to facilitate the goal or function and is usually either:

- Project-based, e.g. hurling a product
- Department or location-based – e.g. your customer service team

BELOW ARE TWO TYPES OF MICROSOFT TEAMS

Public Team

A public team is exposed to anyone in your organization – up to 10,000 people – to join. They don't need someone's endorsement to join it. You can easily change a public team to private, and private to public teams.

Private Team

A private team is for requested members only – the team's owner adds and removes them. Currently, a private team is not detectable to everybody in your organization.

In the future, there will be an alternative to make private teams discoverable – Manage discovery of private teams in Microsoft Teams.

CHAPTER 2

NAVIGATING MICROSOFT TEAMS

DOWNLOADING, INSTALLING AND OPENING TEAMS

1. **Open your preferred web browser and traverse to Microsoft.com.**

2. **Log in using the account badges you created when you register for the Office 365 trial.**

3. **When offered with the alternative to download Teams or use the web app, click the Use the Web App Instead link.**

After logging in, you are accessible with the main Teams app running inside your web browser, as shown below.

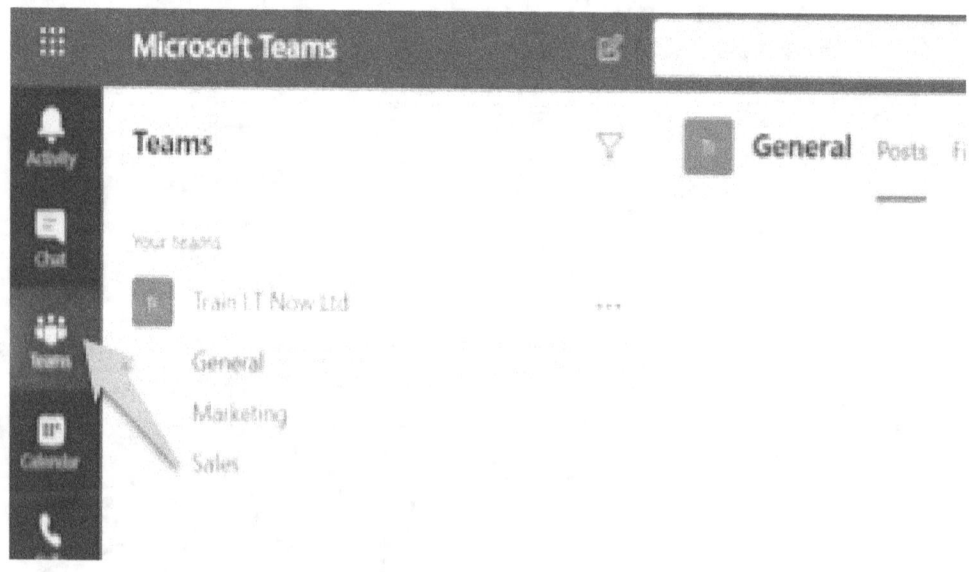

Microsoft Teams running in a web browser.

Many people just use this web-based knowledge to use Teams. Nevertheless, I choose the client that I download and install on my personal computer. I find it has copious more functionality and assimilates better with devices like my headset for phone calls and my webcam for video calls.

To install the Teams client on your Windows laptop or desktop computer, follow the procedure below:

Open your web browser and direct it to Microsoft.com. If you have not signed in to the web app from the preceding set of steps, you are asked to log in. If you have already signed in, you will see the Teams web app presented in your browser.

Log in to the Teams site by entering the identifications you set up in.

When you first sign in to the **Teams site**, you are offered an alternative of installing the Teams client or continuing to the net app. In the preceding set of steps, we continued to the web app. We will install the desktop client.

Click your profile icon that appears in the top-right corner and select Download the Desktop App as shown.

Save the file on your personal computer.

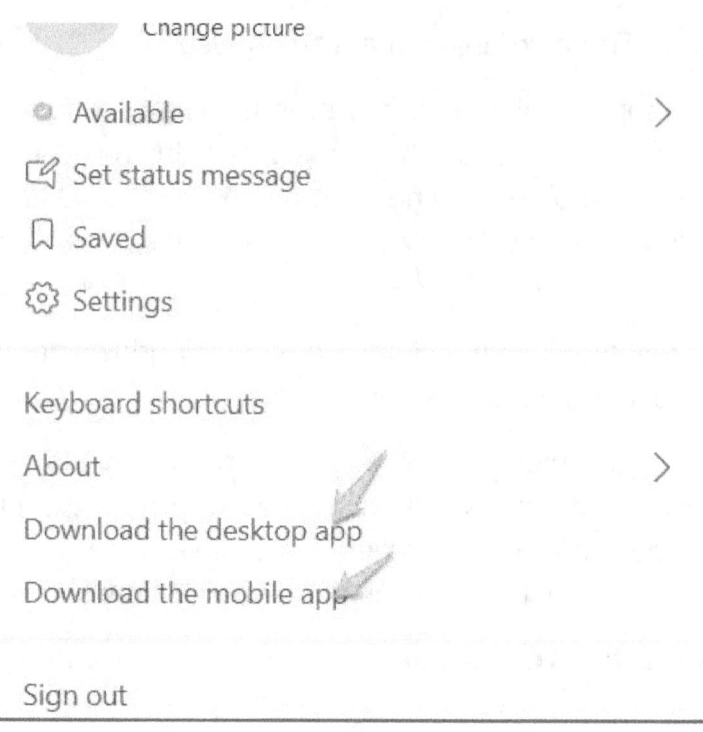

Your profile drop-down menu has options to install the desktop and mobile apps.

You can set the site on your computer's hard drive where your net browser downloads files. By evasion, files are frequently set to download to a Downloads dossier, where all downloads are stowed. If you can't find the file you downloaded, check the configuration for your net browser to see where it stored files it has downloaded.

1. **Once the Teams layout file has been downloaded, open and run the file.**
   After a few moments, a dialog box seems to ask you to sign in, as shown below.

A Login dialog box appears when Teams first installs.

1. **Enter your username and clack Sign In.** If you have signed in previously to Teams using your net browser, you won't be asked for your password again. The Teams user loads and let you know that there is one last phase to get Teams set up and connected to Office, as shown.

One more step to set up Teams with Office

Click **Let's do it**, then click **Yes** in the next screen to get everything hooked up.

Let's do it

A dialog box lets you know Teams will now be connected to Office.

1. **Click let us Do It to continue and then click Yes to permit Teams to make differences to your computer.** Teams work in the background to connect with Office on your computer and then load the Teams application, as shown.

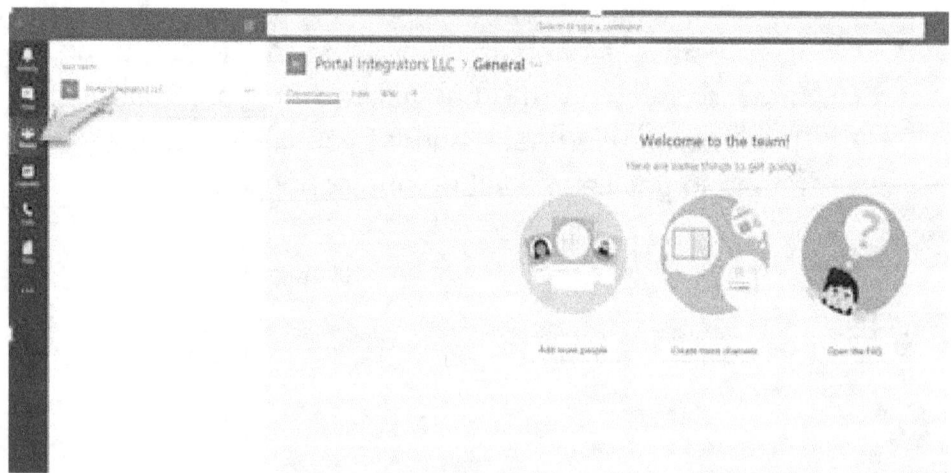

The Teams user running on your personal computer.

TAKING QUICK SPIN AROUND THE TEAMS ACTIVITY

The Teams worker activity report provides insight into the most common events users engage in within Teams. This encompasses metrics such as the number of participants in channel conversations, private chat messages exchanged, and engagement in calls or meetings. These statistics are available for the entire team as well as for individual users.

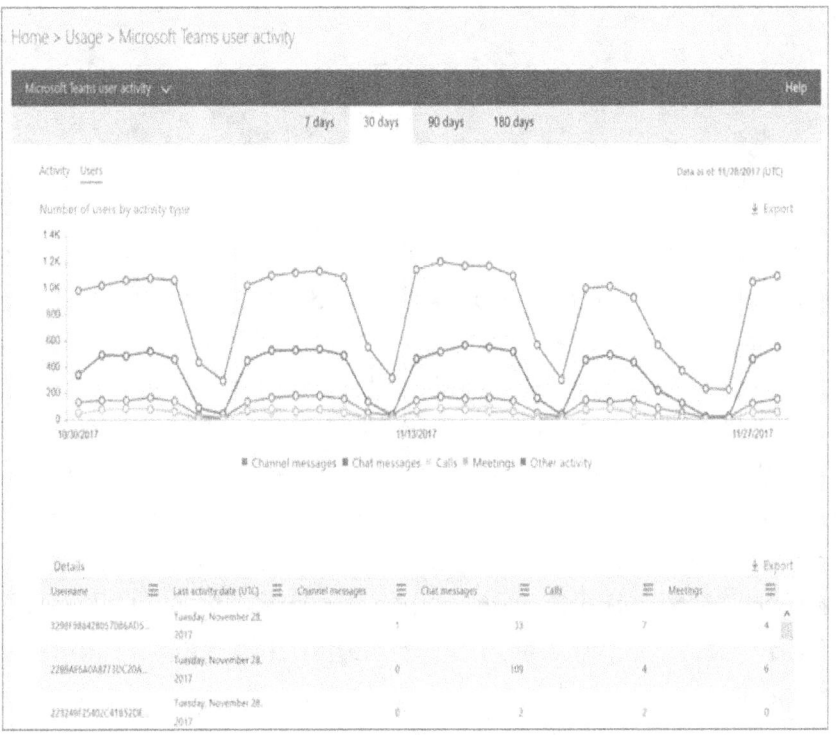

Interpret the Microsoft Teams user activity report

You can get a view of Teams user activity by looking at the **Activity** and **Users** charts.

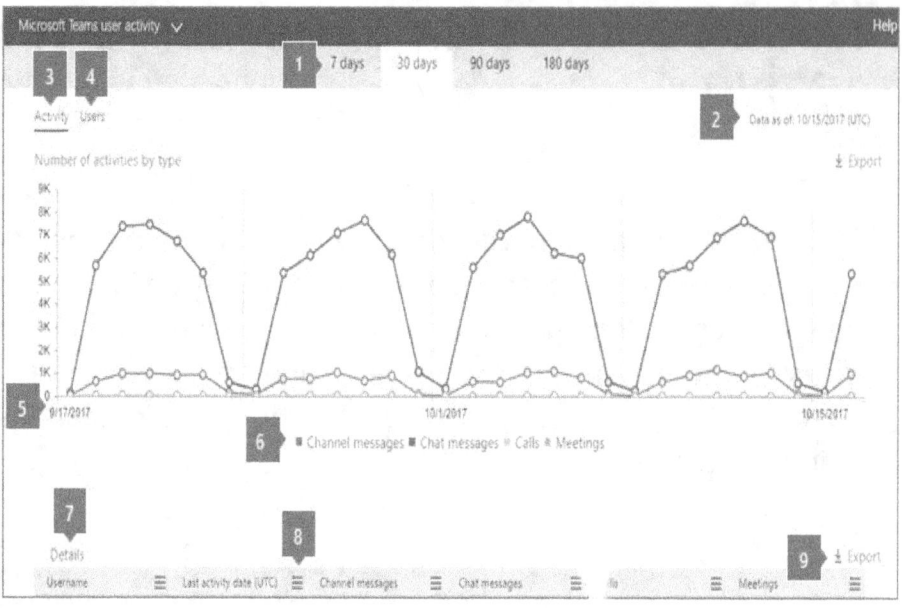

CHAT

Whether your introduction to Microsoft Teams arises from its integration with your group's Office 365 subscription or stems from a personal choice to embrace its functionalities, your initial foray into the platform is likely to involve initiating communications with your team members. In the intricate ecosystem of Microsoft Teams, the heartbeat of instantaneous communication pulsates within its channels. These digital conduits serve as dynamic arenas where individuals converge to exchange ideas, disseminate information through file uploads, and seamlessly share pertinent links. Picture channels as bespoke spaces within a bustling marketplace, each meticulously crafted to cater to specific themes or topics of discussion. They epitomize digital amphitheaters where team members convene to engage in meaningful dialogue, thereby fostering a vibrant sense of camaraderie and collaboration.

Within the expansive framework of Teams, a team constitutes the overarching entity, akin to a collective hub, while channels represent the multifaceted threads interwoven within this cohesive tapestry. This organizational structure provides teams with the flexibility to tailor their digital landscape according to their unique requirements and objectives.

The significance of channel nomenclature cannot be overstated; it serves as the compass guiding team members through the labyrinth of digital discourse. A judiciously chosen name encapsulates the essence and purpose of the channel, acting as a beacon that beckons participants to embark on a journey of discovery and collaboration. For instance, envision establishing a channel dedicated to the nuanced exploration of engineering practices; christening it "Engineering Practice" not only confers clarity but also cultivates a sense of belonging and purpose among its participants, thereby elevating the discourse to new heights of insight and innovation.

A channel can comprehend several conversations happening at a time. To make these strands of conversation easier to track, Teams cluster them together in what is called *threads*. A thread is merely a theme of conversation. When a person types a new mail, it shows in the channel, and any replies to that original message are located beneath. If any person types a dissimilar message for a different subject, it will become its thread and any responses to that message will be grouped under the original message. In the figure, you can see that I am creating a new theme of conversation. If I want to reply to the current topic, I will click the Reply link at the bottom of the thread that starts with "Hello and welcome to the team!"

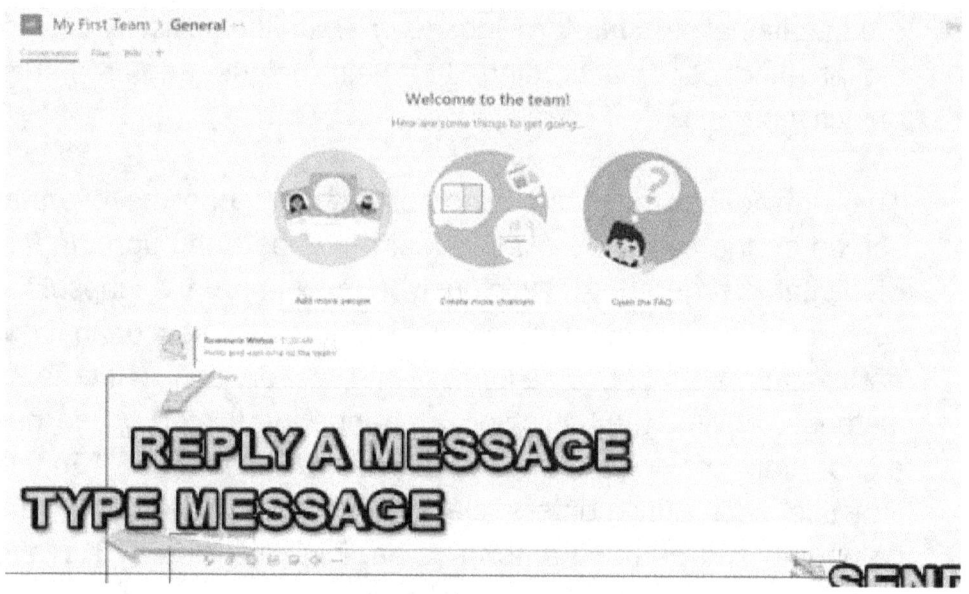

TEAMS

Teams, Microsoft's business messaging application, shares striking similarities with IKEA's self-service units. It functions as an insider's hub, offering a familiar and organized space akin to navigating the aisles and bins of an IKEA store. For those immersed in its workings, such as employees, understanding its organizational structure—such as how aisles and bins are numbered—facilitates seamless navigation. Like a well-versed IKEA shopper effortlessly locating desired items, users of Teams can efficiently access its features once they grasp its layout and functionality. Teams serves as a pivotal tool for connectivity and collaboration, akin to how IKEA's layout aids shoppers in finding desired products. Particularly in the current era of remote work, where many individuals are working from home and connecting with colleagues from afar, mastering platforms like Teams is imperative. Just as IKEA's self-service model revolutionized furniture shopping, Teams and other remote-work collaboration tools have become essential for maintaining productivity and communication in dispersed work environments.

Whether its arrangement agrees with you may set the quality for your relationship with Teams. If it connects, you'll like this chat app for everything else it has to offer, from its long list of assimilation selections to its ability to work effortlessly with any other Microsoft 365 app. Given its potential, Teams is a top teamwork choice, but classically only for clusters already using Microsoft products. That same close-fitting integration that makes it eye-catching to Microsoft customers also means it's not for everybody, remarkably shops that aren't Microsoft-centric.

CALENDER

In modern workplace settings, teams rely on a diverse array of tools aimed at enhancing productivity and fostering seamless communication among team members. Among these tools are text-based chat features, facilitating quick exchanges of messages for efficient collaboration. Additionally, voice and video call capabilities provide avenues for more dynamic and interactive discussions, bridging distances and enabling face-to-face communication regardless of physical location. Furthermore, file-sharing functionalities empower team members to easily exchange documents, presentations, and other essential materials, fostering a collaborative environment where information can be readily accessed and utilized. Task management tools allow for the organization and delegation of responsibilities, ensuring that team objectives are effectively pursued and achieved.

In addition to these core features, online shift records offer a centralized platform for managing work schedules and tracking employee availability, streamlining administrative processes and facilitating coordination within the team. Moreover, the integration of shared calendars within Microsoft Teams stands as a pivotal feature, enabling team members to seamlessly coordinate meetings and events. Through the shared calendar functionality, team members can initiate meetings directly within the Teams application, providing pertinent details such as date, time, agenda, and participant list. By doing so, not only are team members promptly notified of upcoming events, but the events are also automatically synchronized with their respective Microsoft Teams calendars, ensuring visibility and alignment across the entire team.

In essence, Microsoft Teams serves as a comprehensive platform that not only facilitates communication and collaboration but also empowers teams to effectively manage tasks, schedules, and events, thereby enhancing overall productivity and efficiency within the workplace.

How Microsoft Teams Calendars Work

Microsoft Teams is a partnership tool intended for organizations or groups and is thus structured with a group, or team, focus in mind. You may likely sign into a Microsoft Teams group with your steady email, but more often you cannot, you are assigned an enterprise email that you use to access Teams and other related Microsoft 365 apps and services.

The Microsoft Teams app has one key calendar that's allocated to your entire group or association. Group affiliates can add meetings or events to this calendar that automatically appears in the calendar for other members. Individuals can be added to calendar events or meetings if they are required to join.

How to Create a Microsoft Teams Shared Calendar Event

Let's discuss the process for creating an event, which we call a meeting in Microsoft Teams, that can be shared with other group members and automatically added to the group calendar. Below are the steps for creating a shared calendar event in Microsoft Teams:

1. Open the Microsoft Teams app.

2. Select Calendar.
3. Click on New meeting.
4. Choose the appropriate time zone from the drop-down menu at the top of the screen. You don't need to worry about the time zone of your team members as the meeting time will adjust automatically for them.
5. Enter a name for your meeting in the Add title field.
6. In the Add required attendees field, type the names of the people you want to notify about the event. As you type, names should appear for you to select from.
- If you want to share this calendar event with people outside your Microsoft Teams group or who don't use Microsoft Teams, enter their full email address instead of their name.
- Click Optional to include group members who should be informed about the meeting but don't need to attend.
- Once the meeting is created, all invited parties will receive an invitation to their respective email addresses.
7. Specify the start and end times for your meeting.
8. Click Does not repeat from the menu to open options for making the meeting a recurring event if necessary. For example, you may want to schedule this same meeting every weekday, weekly, or monthly.
9. Click Add channel if your meeting is specific to a certain team within your organization's Microsoft Teams setup. For instance, you may want to place it within a Managers channel so that only those team members who use that channel are aware of the meeting.
10. Next is the Add location field. Despite its name, this isn't for specifying a physical location. Instead, it's for selecting a connected Microsoft Teams-enabled Room system.
11. In the large field at the bottom of the screen, provide details for the meeting, such as a description, agenda, or any necessary attachments.

12. Finally, click Send. This will add the event to your Microsoft Teams calendar and invite those you've added. Once they RSVP, the event will be automatically added to their calendars as well.

CALLS

You can make one-on-one or group calls with anybody in your society directly from a chat without having to host a team meeting. These calls are isolated and won't show in any team conversation. Entries for the calls will appear in your chat, though.

1. Go to your chat list, and click **New chat** to start a new conversation.

2. Type the name or names into the **To** field at the top of your new chat.

3. Select **Video call** or **Audio call** to start a call.

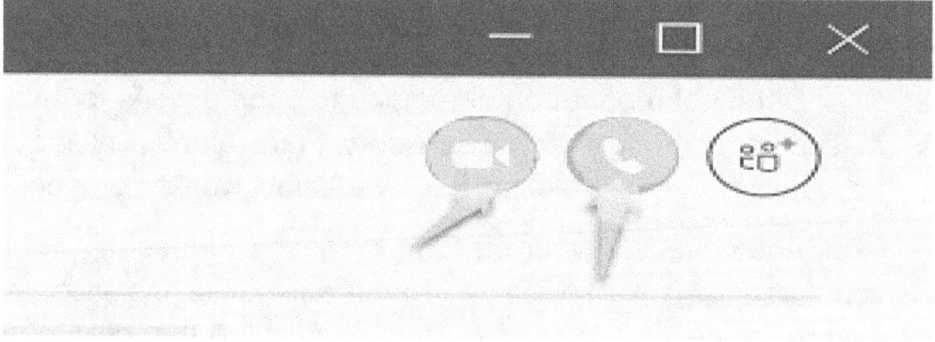

FILES

As your team collaborates, undoubtedly there will be files that you'll need to share and work on together. Teams simplifies this process by providing easy-to-use features for sharing files and collaborating on them collectively. Whether you're working with Word documents, Excel spreadsheets, PowerPoint presentations, or Visio diagrams, your team members can seamlessly view, edit, and collaborate on these files directly within the Teams platform. This integration streamlines workflow and enhances productivity by eliminating the need to switch between different applications or platforms to work on shared files..

Your files library

Within every team there are channels. Think of these channels as a place for your entire team to discuss a particular subject, like impending training, or project updates. Each channel has its file folder where you can share files for that particular channel. To access that folder go to the channel and hand-picked the **Files** tab above the chat window.

In the library, you can upload existing files or create new ones. When you upload a file, it creates a copy in Teams.

Create a file

To create a Word, PowerPoint, or Excel document in Teams, select **New**, then hand-picked the kind of file you like to create. The new file will open in Teams so you can start editing, and if you prefer to work in the desktop version of the app, select **Open in Desktop**

App at the top of the app, at the center of the ribbon. As soon as it is created your new file will be obtainable for your team members to edit as well.

USING TEAMS ACROSS MANY DEVICE AND PLATFORM

You can succeed devices used with Microsoft Teams in your association from the Microsoft Teams administration center. You can sight and manage the device catalog for your association and do jobs such as update, restart, and monitor diagnostics for devices. You can also generate and allocate configuration profiles to a device or group of devices.

To cope with devices, such as change device structure, restart devices, manage updates, or view device and outlying health, you need to be allocated one of the following Microsoft 365 admin parts:

- Microsoft 365 Global admin
- Teams Service admin
- Teams Device admin

CHAPTER 3

STARTING YOUR FIRST TEAM AND MANAGING YOUR SETTINGS

CREATING A NEW TEAMS

If you're starting fresh with a new Microsoft 365 account and haven't yet established a Microsoft 365 group or team, you have the opportunity to create one and tailor its organization to your preferences.

Once you've completed the setup process, you'll receive a corresponding Microsoft 365 group, which comes equipped with a group inbox and calendar accessible through Outlook, a dedicated SharePoint site for collaborative document management, and a OneNote notebook for centralized note-taking.

To initiate the creation of a team from scratch, follow these steps:

1. Begin by navigating to the Teams section located on the left-hand side of the application interface. From there, click on "Join or create a team" located at the bottom of your team's list.

2. Next, click on "Create team," which is typically the first card presented in the top-left corner of the interface.

3. Select the option to "build a team from scratch," indicating your intention to create a customized team environment tailored to your specific needs and preferences.

4. Now, you'll need to specify the nature of your team:

- If you wish to restrict content and communication to a select group of individuals, opt for the "Private" setting.

- Alternatively, if your team is intended to be open to all members of the organization, choose the "Public" setting to encourage broader participation and collaboration.

5. Provide a name for your team and, if desired, include an optional description to provide additional context or information.

6. Once you've finalized the setup details, click on "Create" to proceed with the creation of your team, initiating the process of establishing the associated Microsoft 365 group and its corresponding resources.

This detailed walkthrough should help you navigate the process of building a new team within Microsoft Teams from the ground up, ensuring that it's configured to meet your specific requirements and preferences. Let me know if you need further clarification on any of the steps!

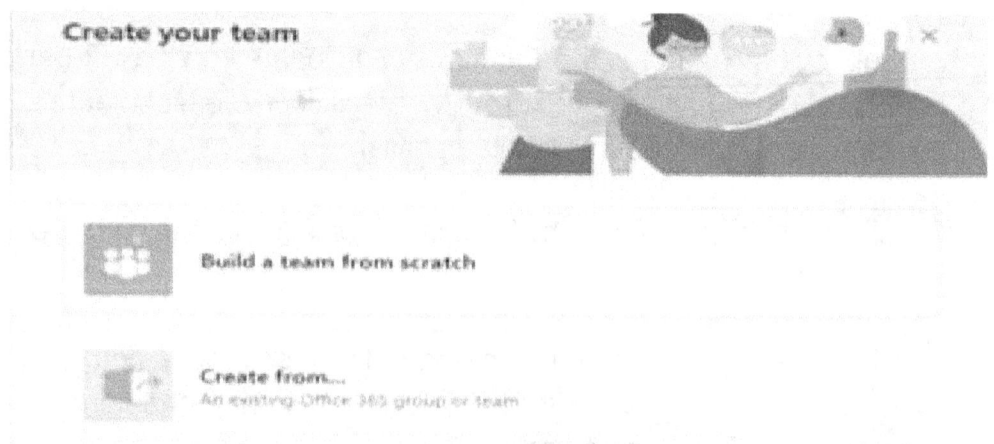

INVITING PEOPLE TO YOUR TEAM

1. Select **Chat** or **Teams** on the left side of the app, then select **Invite people**.

2. Select **Invite your contacts** to pick from your list of email contacts, or select **Invite by email** to physically enter who you want to invite.

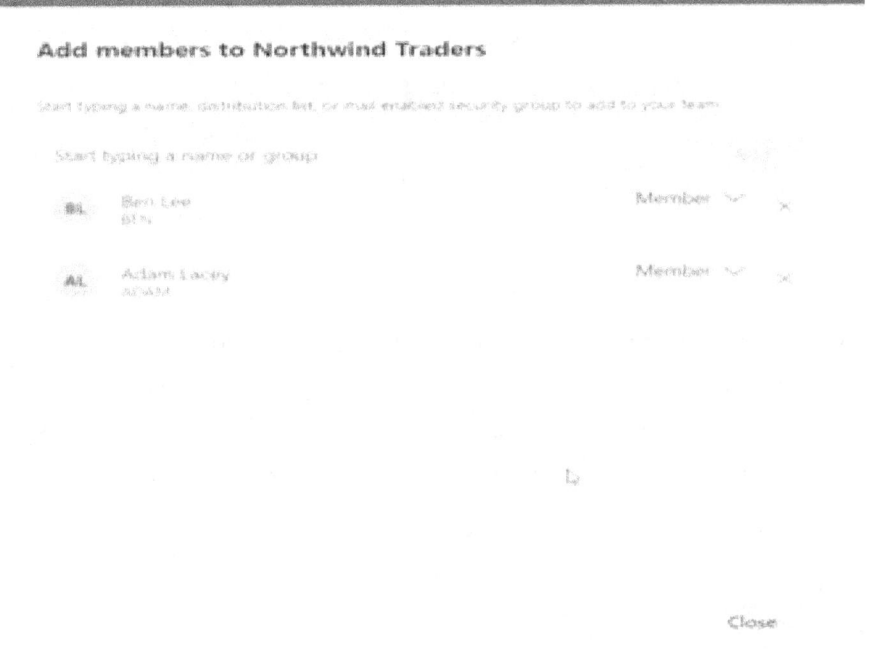

3. Handpicked **Send invites** to send every person an email invitation to join the org.

4. Once they have joined your Team's free org, add them to a precise team you have created.

MANAGING YOUR TEAM SETTINGS

Certainly! As the administrator overseeing various configurations within Microsoft Teams, you play a pivotal role in managing settings tailored to your specific teams' needs. Your responsibilities encompass a range of tasks crucial for smooth collaboration and communication. Here's a detailed breakdown of the key settings you'll frequently utilize:

1. **User Management:**

- **Owners, Members, and Guests:** You're tasked with adding and removing individuals as owners, members, or guests within your Teams environment. Owners have administrative privileges, members actively participate in the team's activities, and guests are external collaborators granted limited access.

2. **Channel Management:**

- **Creating and Deleting Channels:** Channels serve as dedicated spaces for organizing conversations and content around specific topics or projects. You have the authority to create new channels to accommodate evolving needs and delete redundant ones to streamline communication.

3. **Operator Configuration:**

- **Assigning and Adjusting Roles:** Within channels, you can designate operators who possess additional moderation capabilities. These roles empower certain members to manage conversations, moderate content, and enforce chat conduct guidelines effectively.

4. **Chat Conduct:**

- **Enforcing Guidelines:** Upholding appropriate conduct and fostering a respectful environment is paramount. You'll oversee the implementation of chat conduct policies, ensuring that interactions align with organizational standards and promote productive collaboration.

5. **App Integration:**

- **Managing Apps:** Integrating third-party applications enhances Teams' functionality and supports diverse workflows. You'll handle the integration of relevant apps, facilitating seamless access to tools and resources that complement your team's objectives.

By adeptly navigating these settings, you empower your teams to leverage Microsoft Teams as a cohesive platform for communication, collaboration, and productivity. Your proactive management ensures that the environment remains conducive to teamwork, innovation, and success.

Managing your Teams settings

To open the settings for a team, click the elision next to the name of the team to open the more selections drop-down menu and select Manage Team.

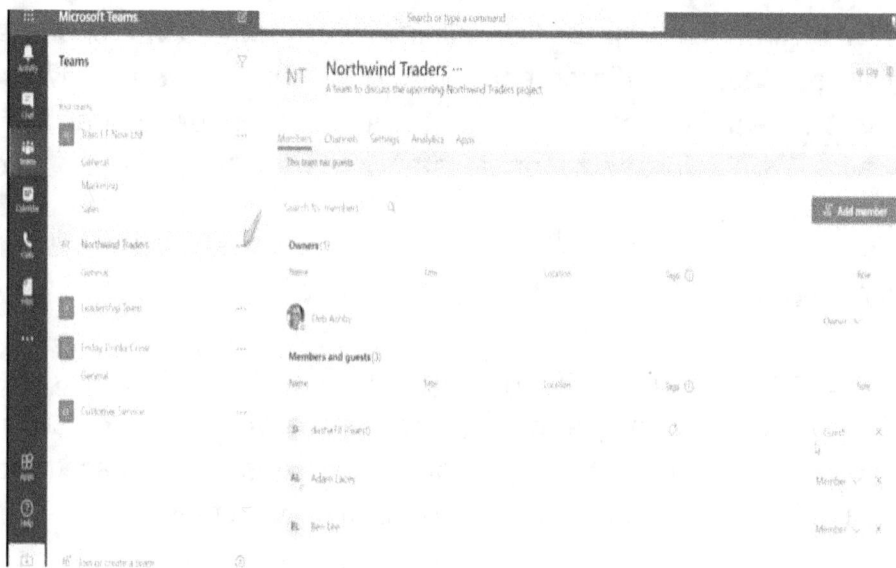

The settings screen for a team comprises the following tabs at the top, as shown below:

- **Members:** The Members screen is where new members are been added to the team. You can add people as members of the team or as guests. A guest *operator* is a user who has access to Teams and can chat with you but does not have access to the rest of your Office 365 environment.

- **Channels:** The Channels screen is where you can add a channel. A *channel* is a zone of a team where you can chat about a mutual theme.

- **Settings:** The Settings screen is where you manage the settings for a team, as shown. On the Settings screen, you can set the team picture, set the approvals of operators including what approvals you want to give to guest operators, set how @mentions work, get a connection to the team that you can share so others can join the team.

33

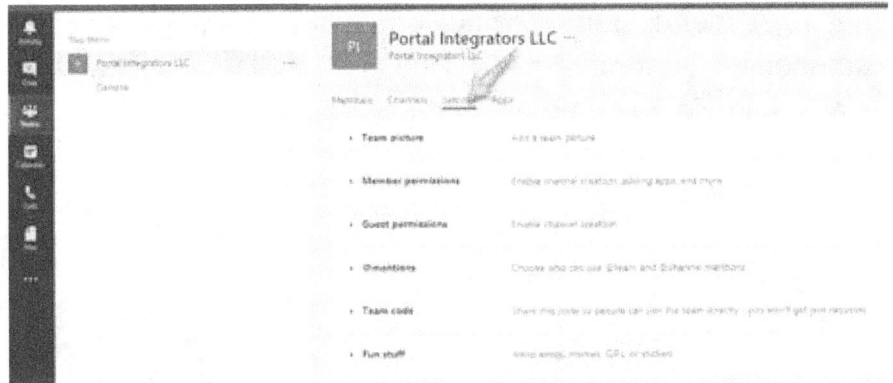

- **Apps:** The Apps screen is where you can add apps to the team. You can see that some apps are installed by evasion. You can add more by clicking the More Apps button.

MANAGING YOUR USER SETTINGS

Several settings are exclusive to each Teams operator. I like to think of these as your user settings; you can think of them as your profile settings. These settings are found in the drop-down menu that appears when you click your profile image in the top-right corner of the Teams window, as shown below.

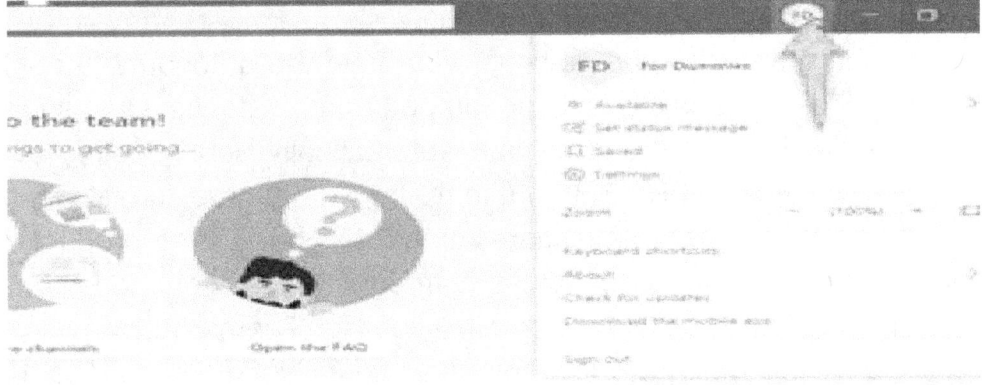

The profile drop-down menu.

When you choose the Settings selection from your profile menu, you can change numerous things that are special to your account. The settings menu, shown here, includes settings for six different categories: General, Privacy, Notifications, Devices, Permissions, and Calls. I provide a summary of these sections here.

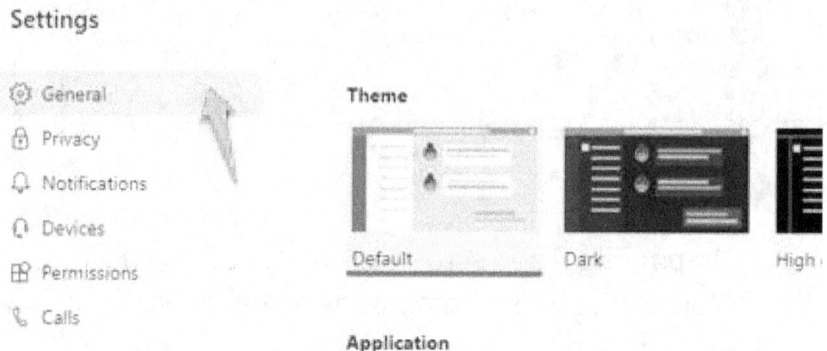

General

The "Overall" section encompasses a variety of settings that shape the experience within your chosen subject, dictate the functionality of the application, and define the semantic preferences you wish to employ. Tailoring the appearance of the Teams interface is made possible by adjusting the subject you select. For instance, you might opt for a high-contrast theme over the default setting, thus customizing the visual aesthetic to suit your preferences.

Within the application settings, you have the autonomy to configure how Teams behaves on your computer. For instance, you can specify whether Teams should initiate automatically upon booting up your system. Additionally, within this realm, you can designate Teams as the primary chat application across all your Office products. This feature proves particularly advantageous in scenarios where an organization transitions from Skype to Teams, allowing you to seamlessly integrate Teams into your workflow as the default communication platform. Furthermore, you have the flexibility to modify language settings and keyboard arrangements to align with your preferred linguistic and typing conventions. This ensures a personalized and efficient user experience tailored to your specific needs and preferences.

Privacy

Within the Privacy unit of the system, users have access to a range of customizable settings aimed at enhancing control over their interactions and communications. These settings encompass features such as primacy access, read receipts, and surveys, each designed to tailor the user experience to individual preferences.

Primacy access serves as a means of specifying who is granted priority access to reach out to the user, particularly when their status is set to "Do Not Disturb." This feature allows users to designate certain contacts, such as supervisors or key collaborators, who are permitted to bypass the default settings and contact them even when they are in a state of limited availability. For instance, while the user may wish to receive emails from their superior at any time, they may prefer that all other contacts wait until their status is set to "Available."Read receipts offer users the option to notify senders when they have read their emails. This feature can be toggled on or off based on personal preferences. If a user wishes to maintain privacy and not disclose when they have viewed a message, they have the ability to disable read receipts.

Additionally, users have the option to enable or disable surveys within the platform. Surveys serve as a tool utilized by Microsoft to gather feedback and insights aimed at improving Teams. Users can choose to leave this feature enabled if they are willing to provide responses to surveys. However, for those who prefer not to engage with surveys or be prompted for feedback, they have the option to disable this feature. By turning off surveys, users can ensure that Microsoft does not solicit their input for the purpose of refining the Teams experience according to their feedback.

Notifications

In the Notifications section, you have the ability to personalize how Microsoft Teams notifies you about various events. You can specify which actions trigger notifications to appear in your banner and be sent via email, limit notifications to appear solely in your Activity feed, or opt to disable them entirely. This customization empowers you to tailor your Teams experience to suit your preferences and work style effectively.

Devices

It seems like you're asking about configuring devices for use with Microsoft Teams. In Microsoft Teams, you can adjust settings related to your audio, video, and other hardware devices to ensure a smooth experience during meetings and calls. Here's a breakdown of how you can manage your devices in Teams:

Accessing Device Settings:

Open Microsoft Teams on your computer or mobile device.

Click on your profile picture or initials in the top right corner.

From the dropdown menu, select "**Settings**".

Audio Settings:

Click on the "**Devices**" tab. Here you'll find settings related to your audio devices.

Under the "**Speaker**" section, you can choose the audio output device you want to use during meetings. This could be your computer speakers or a headset.

In the "**Microphone**" section, select the microphone you want Teams to use. You can test your microphone to ensure it's working properly by speaking into it and observing the volume indicator. Adjust the speaker and microphone volume levels using the sliders provided.

Video Settings:

If you have a webcam or built-in camera, you can configure it under the "**Camera**" section.

Choose your preferred camera device from the dropdown menu. If you have multiple cameras connected to your device, you can select the one you want to use. Test your camera to make sure it's working correctly by observing the video preview.

Additional Settings:

Depending on your device and Teams version, you may have additional settings related to phone or headset configuration. These settings allow you to choose your preferred communication device for making and receiving calls.

Saving Changes:

Once you've configured your devices to your liking, make sure to click "**Save**" or "Apply" to save your changes.

By adjusting these settings, you can ensure that your audio and video devices are properly configured for Microsoft Teams meetings and calls, providing you with the best possible experience during communication and collaboration sessions.

Permissions

You can turn permissions on or off for Teams in this unit. For example, do you like Teams to be capable to use your location or be able to open peripheral links in your net browser? You organize those permissions here.

Calls

Teams offer a full voice clarification. It implies that Teams can exchange your regular telephone. In this unit, you can organize how incoming calls are answered as well as setting up and organizing your voicemail and ringtones.

Settings

- General
- Privacy
- Notifications
- Devices
- Permissions
- Calls

Theme

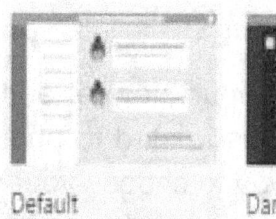  

Default   Dark   High

Application

CHAPTER 4

STAYING CONNECTED TO OTHERS WITH CHANNELS AND CHAT

CHATTING IN TEAMS

Whether prompted by your organization's integration with Microsoft 365 or Office 365, or simply driven by personal choice, Microsoft Teams may become a pivotal tool in your workflow. Upon initiation, your initial interactions within Teams are likely to involve communicating with other members of your team.

In the realm of Teams, immediate correspondence takes place within channels. These channels serve as dynamic spaces where individuals can engage in various forms of communication, including messaging, file sharing, and link dissemination. They represent hubs of collaboration, where colleagues convene to exchange ideas, disseminate information, and foster camaraderie. Within these channels, you embark on a journey of connectivity, seizing opportunities to engage with peers, glean insights, and cultivate a sense of community within your professional network.

A channel subsists inside of a team, and a team can comprehend numerous channels. You can name a channel anything you want. I prefer using a name that labels the drive of the channel. For instants, you can name your channels channelA1, channelA2, etc. The reason for creating the channel will determine the name given to it. A channel was created to discuss sport? Name the channel sports news. A channel was created to discuss on Mechanical Engineering project? You can name the channel Mechanical project. You get the fact.

A channel can comprehend numerous chats occurring simultaneously. To try to make these filaments of chat easier to follow, Teams crowds them together in what is known as *threads.* A thread is simply a theme of the chat. When someone types a new message, it shows in the channel, and any responses to that original chat are placed beneath. If someone else forms a dissimilar message for a dissimilar topic, it will be its thread and any replies to that mail will be clustered under the original message. An example is shown below.

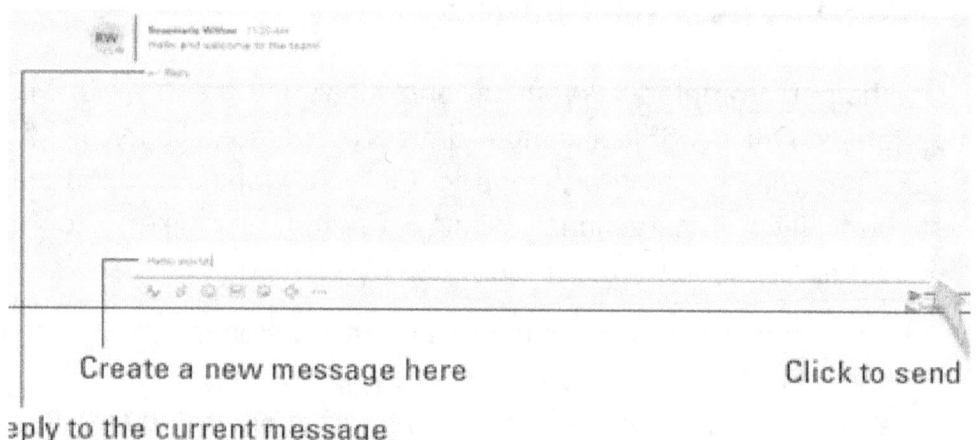

Create a new message here   Click to send

eply to the current message

SENDING MESSAGES IN CHANNELS

When new teams are created, a channel is created for that team robotically. Named "General," this channel is impeccably acceptable to use to start a conversation with others on the team.

To send a mail-in to the General channel, follow these steps below:

1. **Select the Teams icon in the left navigation panel to sight all your teams.**
   Under each team, you will see a list of channels that are obtainable to you. If it is a fresh team, you will only see the General channel until other channels are created.

In addition to the channels obtainable to you, there may be private channels in the team that you can't access. There can also be unrestricted channels, but that you have not joined.

2. **Select the General channel, as shown.** When you clack a channel, it opens in the key part of the screen.

3. **Type a message in the text box at the bottom of the screen and click the Send icon, as shown earlier.** Your note appears on the General channel screen.

Notification above your message that Microsoft Teams is giving you some clues about adding additional people, creating more channels, and opening the Recurrently Asked Questions (RAQ). The buttons which appear in fresh channels are shortcuts for you. You can attain these same responsibilities without using these shortcuts, and you will find out how in the next units.

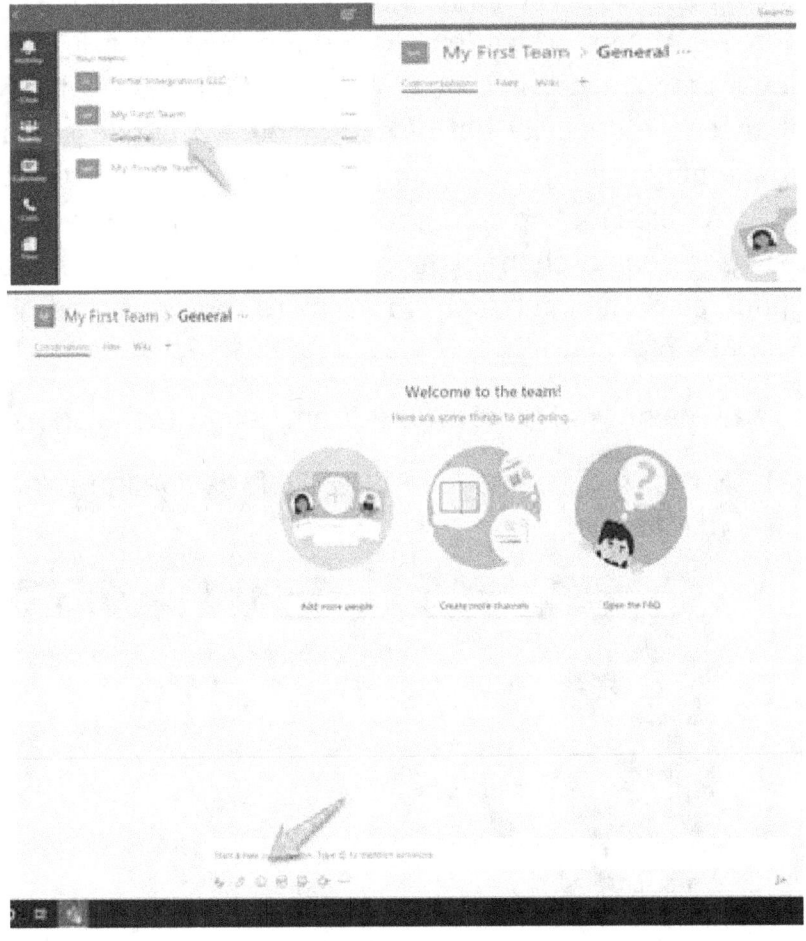

Choosing the General channel that was robotically created when the Team was created.

CREATING A NEW CHANNEL

As you engage with Teams consistently, you'll find the need to establish conversation channels tailored to various themes, ensuring that discussions don't get lost in a single "general" channel. For instance, you might consider setting up channels dedicated to different topics such as sports, mechanics, or team morale occasions. The beauty of Teams lies in its flexibility, allowing you to organize team conversations in seemingly endless ways. What truly matters is finding the approach that best suits the dynamics and needs of your team. By creating specialized channels, you provide a structured environment where team members can delve deeper into specific subjects, share relevant resources, and foster collaboration effectively. This not only enhances productivity but also promotes a sense of cohesion and engagement within the team. So, whether it's brainstorming new ideas, troubleshooting technical issues, or simply boosting team spirit, having dedicated channels ensures that every conversation finds its rightful place, contributing to a more efficient and vibrant team environment.

To create a new channel in your team, follow these steps:

1. Select the Teams icon in the left navigation pane to sight all your teams.

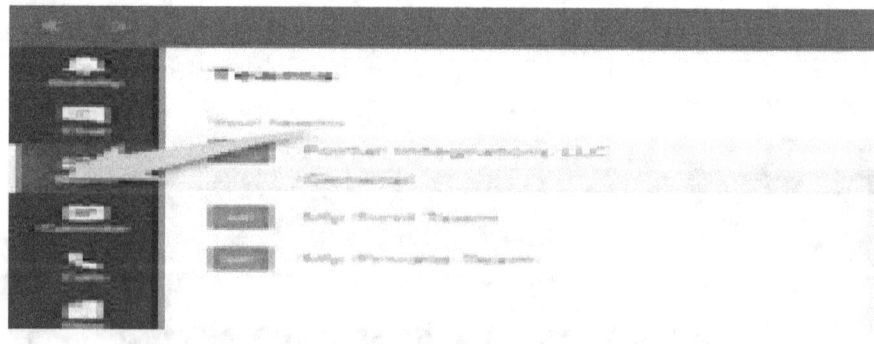

2. Click the elision to the right of the team you wish to add a channel to open the More Alternatives drop-down menu.

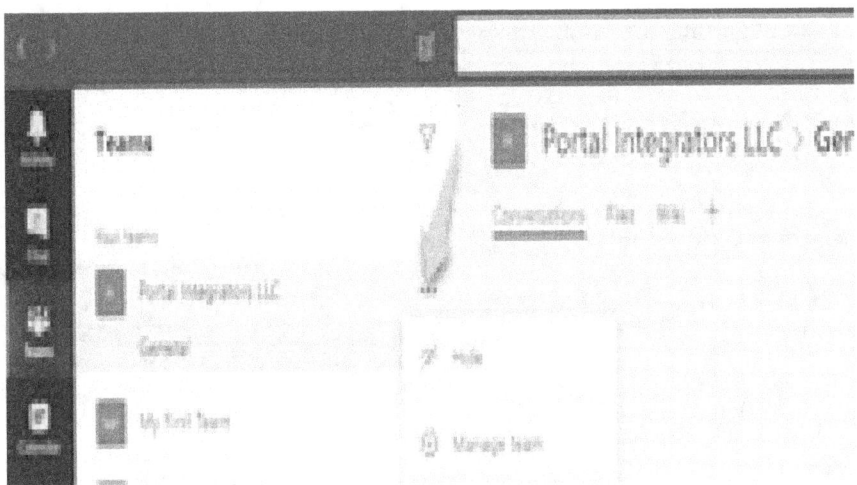

3. Select "**Add channel**", as shown.

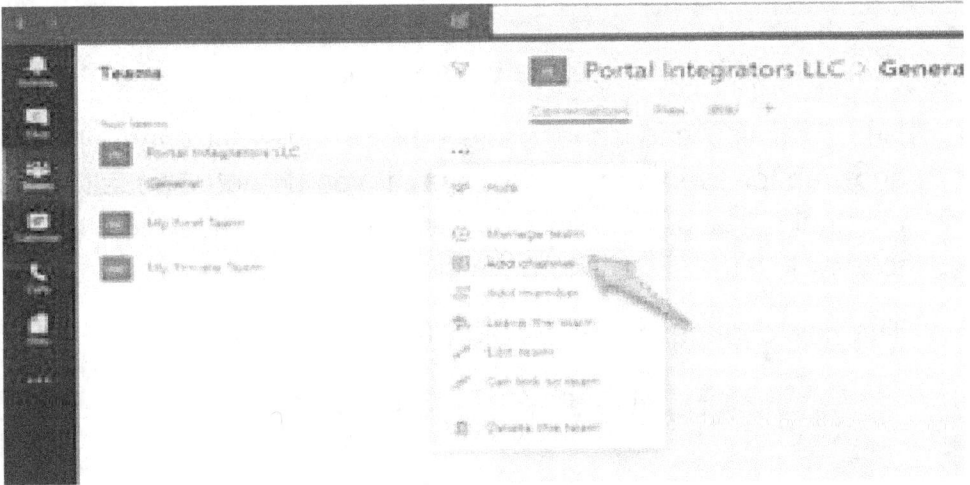

If this alternative isn't shown in the drop-down menu, you don't have the authorization to create a new channel. If you are a guest to a team, your capability to create teams and channels can be restricted.

Choosing Add channel from the settings menu for a team.

4. **Enter a name and depiction for the channel in the dialog box that appears and then clicks Add, as shown below.**

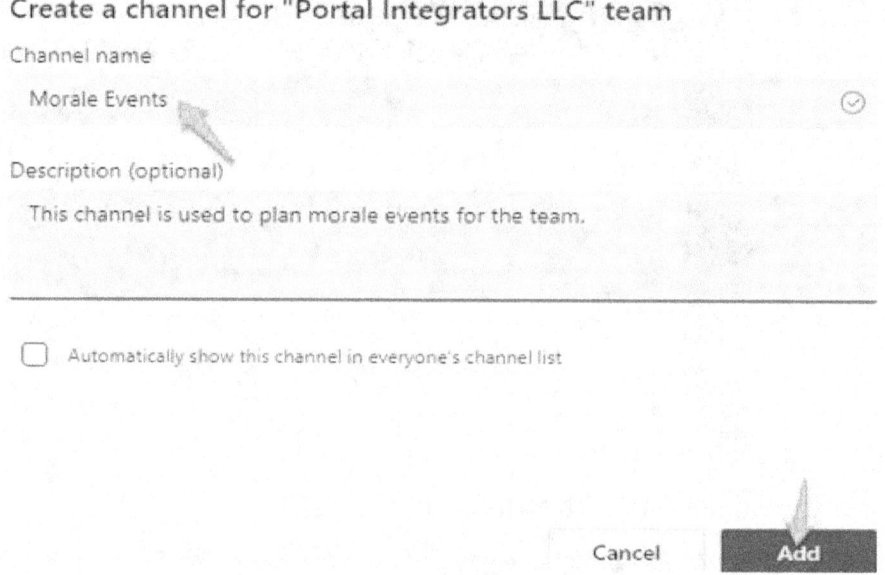

Fill in the dialog box to create a new channel.

Note that you can choose the box to have this channel robotically show up for everybody in the team. If you do not choose this box, the channel will appear as hidden, and people will have to click a button to view it in the list of channels in the team.

The new channel appears below the team as shown.

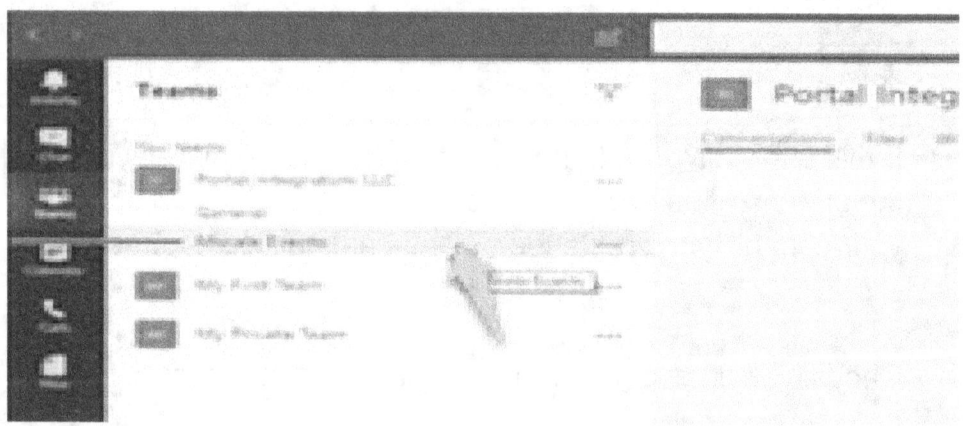

A new channel in a team.

Imagine having the ability to tailor conversation channels to suit any theme or topic of interest. Picture teams achieving remarkable success by segregating their core work-related discussions from more informal, non-core topics. This separation allows for focused discussions on crucial matters, like budget planning, in one channel, while fostering team morale through dedicated channels for events and social gatherings.

In this setup, a channel serves as an integral component of a team's collaboration space. Teams have the flexibility to create multiple channels, each dedicated to a specific subject or area of interest. Within these channels, team members engage in threaded discussions, facilitating organized and efficient communication. By creating distinct channels, teams can maintain clarity and efficiency in their discussions, ensuring that important work-related matters receive the attention they deserve, while also providing space for camaraderie and community-building among team members. This structured approach to communication fosters productivity, teamwork, and a positive work environment.

CONFIGURING A CHANNEL

Several dissimilar settings is been configure for a channel through the More Alternatives dialog box. As shown previously, you access these extra options by clicking the elision next to the channel name you desire to manage. The following figure shows the Additional Options drop-down menu that appears next to the new channel we created. The alternatives that appear for a channel you add include the following:

- **Channel notifications:** You can configure the notifications you receive for this channel. This is significant as your establishment's use of Teams surges. Teams can rapidly become raucous with everybody chatting about all kinds of subjects. This setting can be used to turn down the sound for channels that are less significant to you and turn up the volume for topics to which you need to give more attention. The channel notifications dialog box is shown below.

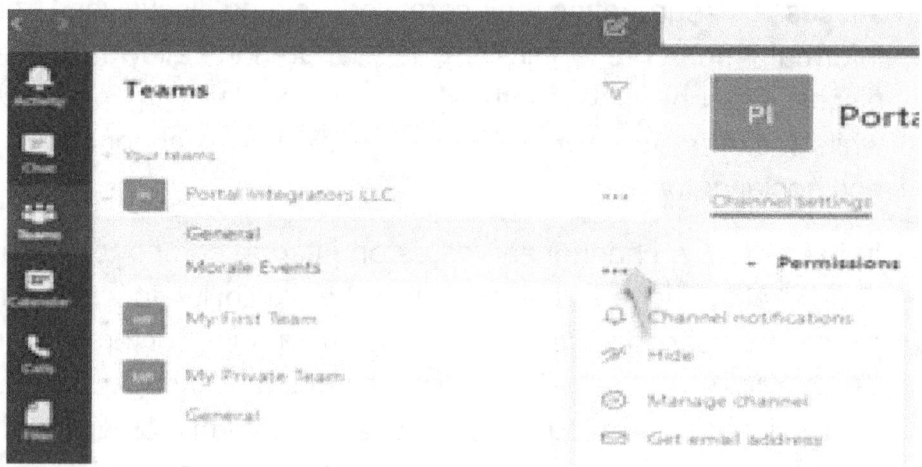

The More Options menu for a team's channel.

Setting channel notifications.

- **Hide:** choose this alternative to hide the channel from various channels you have in the team. You can unhide the channel at any time that pleases you. You will see a mail that will let you know the number of channels you have hidden, and you can click it to see those hidden channels.

- **Manage channel:** This alternative permits the possessors of the channel to manage the permissions for the channel. You can permit others to restrain the channel and control who can post new mails to the channel.

- **Get email address:** A feature that I use all the time is the capability to send an email message straight to a channel. The channel can be configured so that if you send an email, the message appears in the channel.

- **Get a link to the channel:** You can rapidly get incredulous with the number of teams and channels in your association. When you want to inform people about a channel, you can send them a direct link to the channel. You can get the link by using this option.

- **Edit this channel:** When the channel was created initially, you set the title and description. You can transform those settings with this alternative.

- **Connectors:** Connectors are add-on applications. Consider them as practice delays to Teams that you can add to a channel to get connected with other software services. They permit you to unite other apps to your channel. There are numerous types of connectors.

- **Delete this channel:** When you are prepared to eliminate a channel, you can select this alternative to deleting it.

MOVING FROM A CHANNEL TO A CHAT

Navigating the various avenues of connection available within Microsoft Teams can sometimes feel like trying to find your way through a maze. Let's simplify it: think of a team as a gathering of individuals with a common purpose, like a department or project group. Within each team, you'll find channels, which are essentially ongoing conversations or topics relevant to that team's focus. It's akin to different rooms in a house where discussions on various subjects take place. Here's where it gets interesting: you can belong to multiple teams, each with its own set of channels, fostering collaboration across different projects or areas of interest. So, in essence, Teams offers a structured yet flexible environment for communication and collaboration, allowing you to seamlessly engage with colleagues across various teams and channels.

The important thing about this system of communication is that it is well organized. You can choose a team from the left steering pane and see the channels in that team. However, you may also need to fair chat with someone or with groups of people, and you don't want to go through the procedure of setting up a fresh team or channel. Teams have you enclosed with an idea called to *chat*. You find the Chat sign in the left navigation pane just above the Teams sign, as shown below.

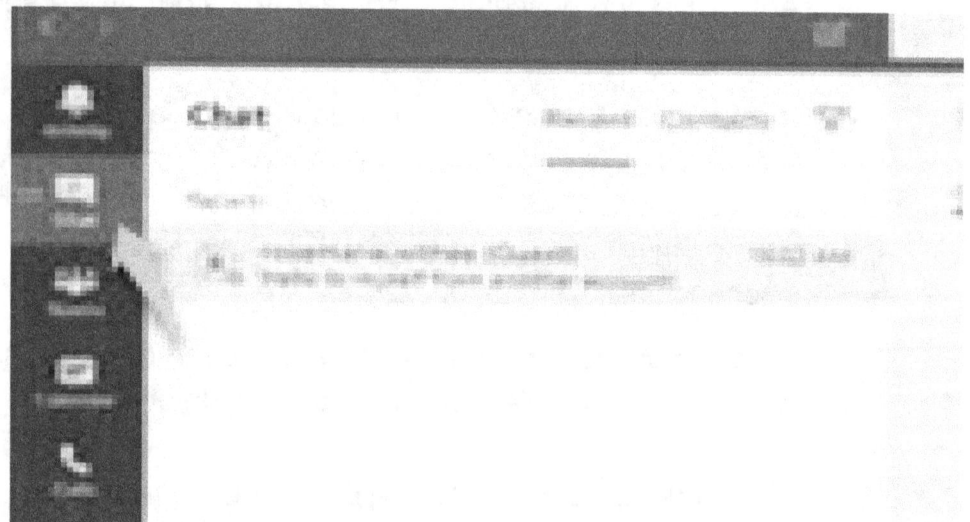

The Chat feature of Teams.

A chat is a regular conversation between two or more people.

Click the Chat icon to view a list of all your open chats. If you recall using AOL Instant Messenger, Skype, or most any other chat application, you may identify that each chat article is like a window.

However, as an alternative to a new window for each chat, each chat appears as an item in the list. Click a chat and you see the key window revive to show that chat.

STARTING A PRIVATE CHAT

You can start an isolated chat by choosing the New Chat icon, which is positioned above the Filter icon at the top of the chat list. The new chat icon airs like a piece of paper with a pencil on it. When you choose the icon, a new chat appears on the right side of the Teams workstation. You type in the name of the person you want to send a chat mails to in the field and click that person's name to add the person to the chat. Once the person has been added to the chat, you can send a message just like it is done in a channel. You type your mail in the text box at the bottom of the chat region and press the Enter key or select the Send icon, which looks like a paper airplane.

The chat icon is shown below

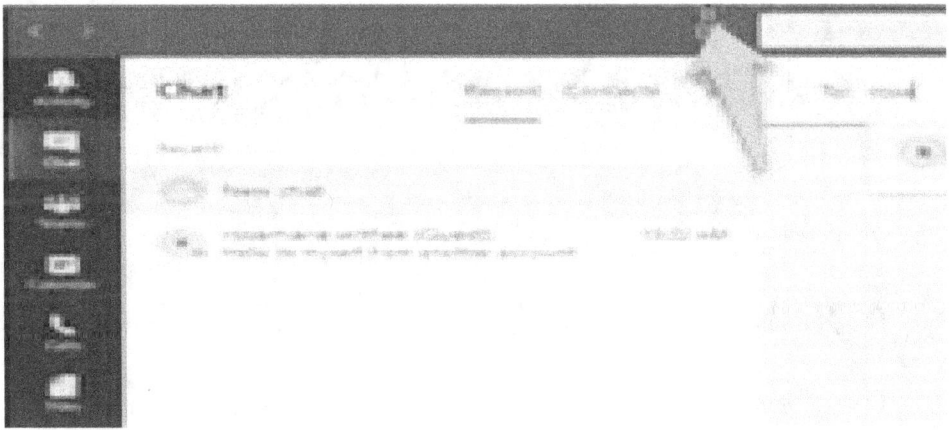

A new chat icon is shown

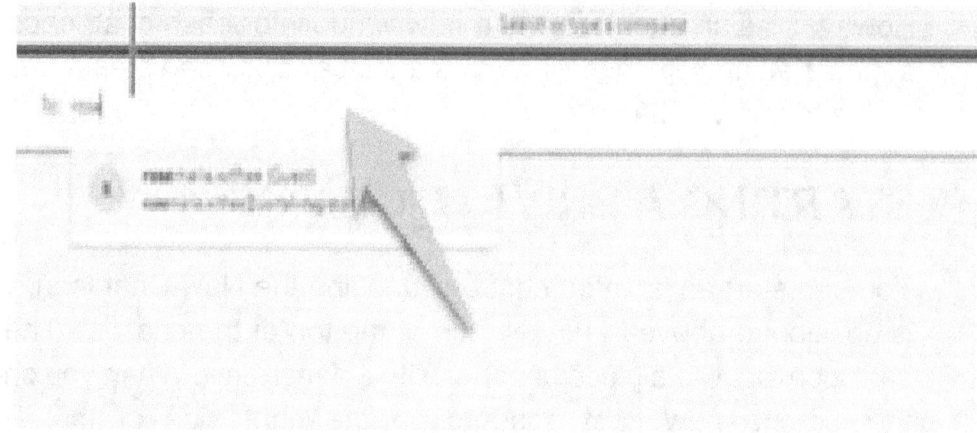

Send icon

Starting a new chat in Teams.

ADDING MULTIPLE PEOPLE TO A CHAT

The previous section delves into the nuances of initiating a fresh conversation. It elucidates the process of engaging with multiple individuals by including them in the initial line when commencing the conversation. Conversely, there may arise situations where you feel the need to incorporate additional participants into an ongoing chat.

To add extra people to the conversation that has already started, choose the Add People icon that appears in the top-right corner of the conversation window. Then, type the names of the people you need to add in the Add dialog box. If you are chatting with a single person and you add another person, a new conversation will show with the three people in the chat. If you have three people already in a chat and you add a fourth person (or more), you will be offered the alternative of including the conversation history for the new people you are adding, as shown below.

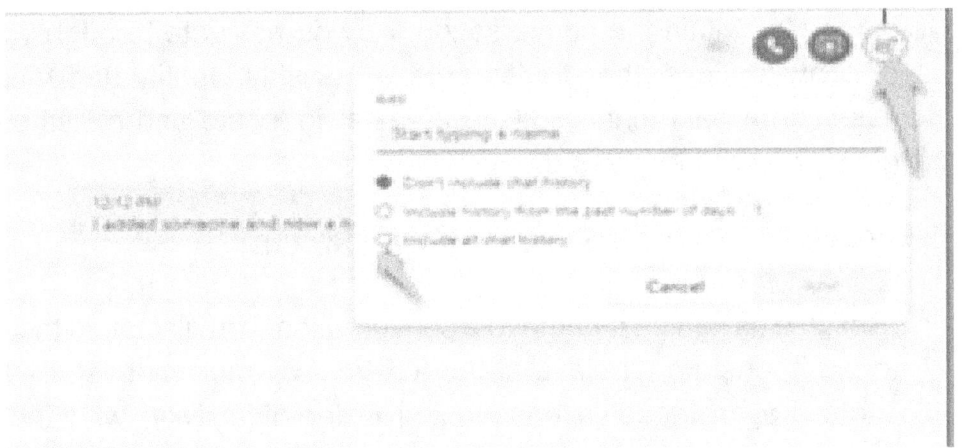

Adding additional people to a chat.

Certainly! When engaging in a conversation with one individual, you're unable to introduce additional participants and maintain the chat history with the new participant. This functionality becomes accessible only when there are at least three individuals involved in the conversation. Microsoft has implemented this feature with privacy considerations in mind. Essentially, if a private conversation is ongoing, Teams ensures that one participant cannot unilaterally share that private discussion with others. This safeguard underscores Microsoft's commitment to maintaining the confidentiality of communication within Teams, fostering a secure and trusted environment for collaboration.

GIVING A CHAT A TITLE

When a conversation starts in a messaging app, it gets listed in your chat history along with the names of the participants. Over time, especially as more people join in, the conversation can evolve and take on a life of its own. It becomes a bustling hub of messages, ideas, and interactions, often revolving around a central theme or topic.

In such cases, it's incredibly useful to assign a title to the chat. This title serves as a quick reminder of the main theme or subject matter discussed within the conversation. As you navigate through your list of conversations, these titles help you swiftly identify and recall the essence of each chat, making it easier to locate and revisit specific discussions when needed.

PINNING A CHAT TO THE TOP OF THE LIST

"Besides assigning a name to a conversation, you also have the option to pin it, ensuring it stays at the forefront of your chat list. Typically, chats are arranged in descending order of activity, with the most recent ones appearing at the top. However, pinning a chat overrides this arrangement, ensuring quick access to a specific conversation, even if it's been dormant for a while without any recent messages. This feature proves invaluable for swiftly navigating to essential conversations, regardless of their recent activity status."

To pin a chat, choose the elision next to the chat in the left navigation panel and select Pin from the More Alternatives drop-down menu, as shown below.

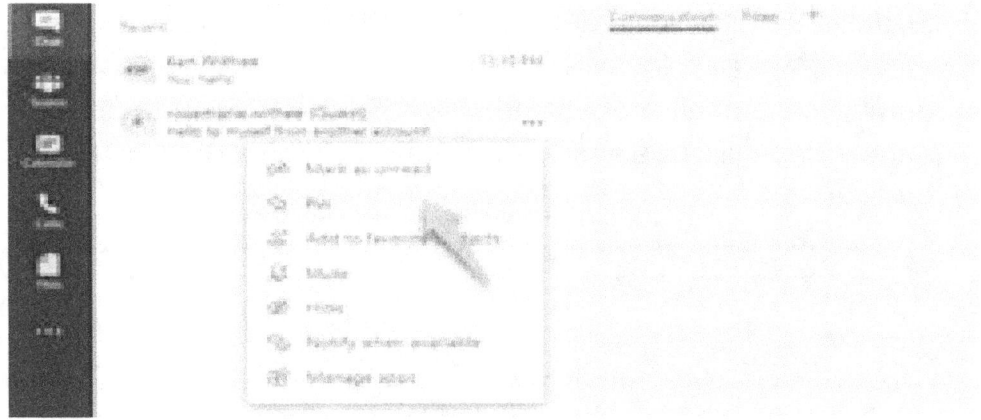

Pinning a chat to the top of the list for quick access.

SENDING MORE THAN TEXT WHEN CHATTING

Typing text into a **Microsoft Teams** channel or chat is the most corporate way of sending your mails to others on the team. However, you could send more than just text. You can send emojis, GIFs, stickers, and even attach files. These options are shown at the bottom of the text box where you type in your message, as shown below.

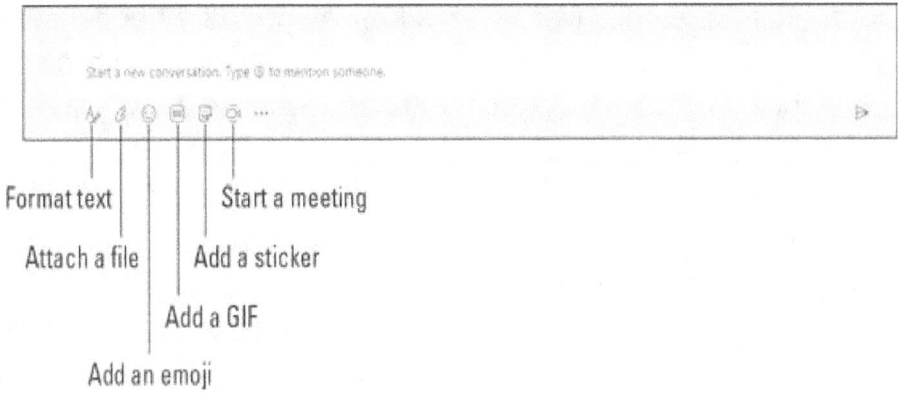

Additional chat options.

ADDING EMOJIS, GIFs, AND STICKERS

Emojis are little icons that show a reaction. For example, a smiling face shows happiness and a sad face shows sadness. You will find emoji icons of all shapes and sizes and meanings. You can send an emoji by clicking the emoji icon and then choosing the emoji you prefer to use.

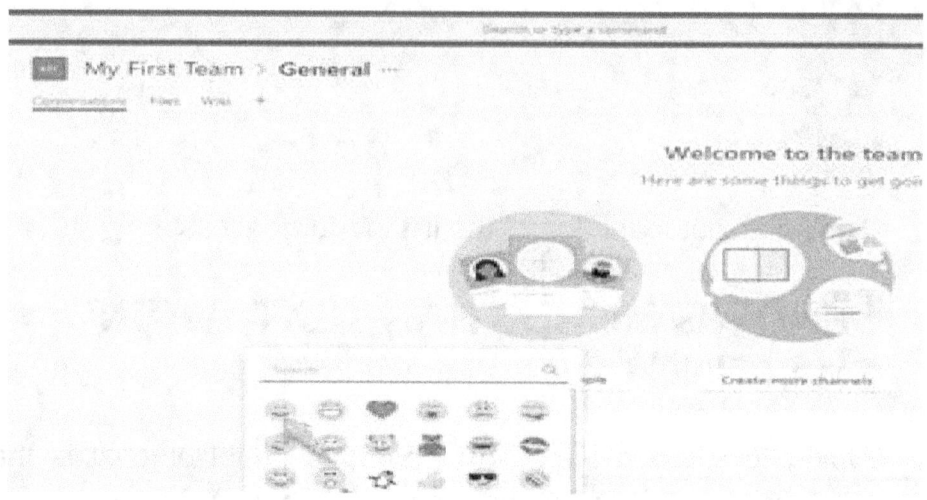

Adding an emoji to your message.

In Microsoft Teams, enhancing your communication with expressive elements like emojis and GIFs is both fun and efficient. Let's delve into the realm of emojis first. Teams has integrated a handy text shortcut system, allowing you to effortlessly summon emojis while typing. For instance, if you're feeling cheerful and want to convey that emotion, simply type a colon followed by a closing parenthesis, and voilà! A happy face emoji magically appears in your message. This intuitive feature eliminates the need to manually browse through a list of emojis, streamlining your communication process. Moreover, you can take it a step further by incorporating keywords enclosed in parentheses to conjure specific emoji icons, ensuring that your messages are as expressive as you intend them to be.

Now, let's talk about GIFs—the dynamic, animated pictures that inject life and humor into your conversations. Within Teams, you have access to a vast library of GIFs encompassing a wide range of themes and emotions. Whether you're in need of a cute cat yawning or a reaction GIF from your favorite television show, Teams has you covered. The process of incorporating these animated snippets into your chat messages is delightfully simple. Just click on the GIF icon located at the bottom of the text box, and a world of animated possibilities awaits you. This feature not only adds a playful dimension to your conversations but also fosters a sense of camaraderie and engagement among team members.

In essence, Microsoft Teams empowers you to express yourself creatively and efficiently through a rich tapestry of emojis and GIFs. So go ahead, sprinkle some emojis and GIFs into your chats, and watch as your communication comes alive with vibrancy and personality. Stickers are short little comic strip–type images. For instants, a drawing with a tongue balloon over the person. Microsoft Teams embraces a lot of popular stickers, and you can add your own as well. Adding a sticker to your message is shown below.

Adding a sticker to your message.

Adding a file

You can also add a file to the chat message. For example, you may be working on an Excel spreadsheet and you prefer to include it in the chat. You can add the file to your chat mails using the paperclip icon, you can select a current file you have been working on, browse the files already uploaded to Teams, select a file from OneDrive, or upload a file from your personal computer.

When you attach a file to a channel, the file is shown in the Files tab at the top of the channel. The Files tab is a SharePoint spot behind the scenes. You can plug the Files tab at the top of the figure in between the chat tab and the Wiki tab.

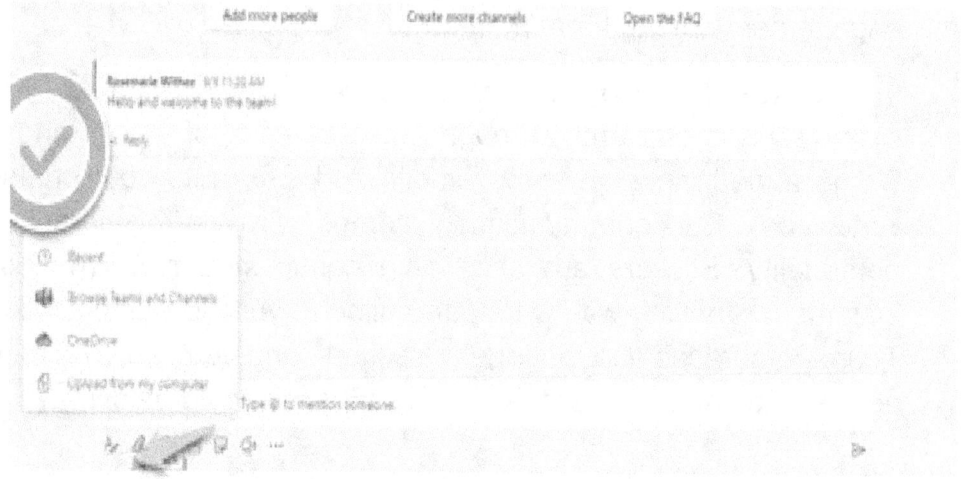

Attaching a file to a message to send to a channel.

Reacting to chat messages

When someone types a message, you can react to it instead of responding to it. To *react* to a message means to acknowledge you have seen the chat. For example, you can react with an emoji such as a thumbs down, a surprise emoji, or many more. To react to a message, you either soar your mouse over the message or choose the elision if you are using a mobile device and touch screen and then select the reaction. In the following figure, I am reacting to a message with a thumbs-up emoji to designate that I like the message and recognize it.

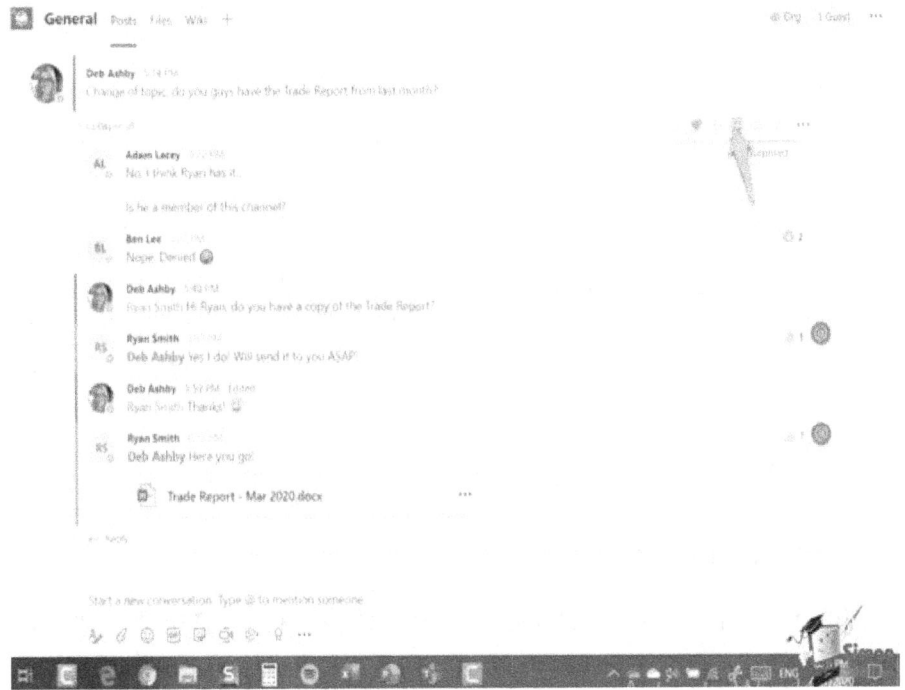

Reacting to a message with a thumbs up.

When someone else has already expressed a reaction, such as a thumbs-up, your subsequent reaction will increment the count of that particular reaction. For example, if your colleague has given a thumbs-up to a message, and you also react with a thumbs-up, a small number "2" will appear next to the thumbs-up emoji. This feature allows for acknowledging a message without the need to type out a reply. It emphasizes the significance of reactions in communication, enabling quick and efficient interaction within the platform.

CHAPTER 5

EXTENDING TEAMS WITH APPS

DISCOVERING APPS ALREADY INSTALLED

THE FILE TAB

Your files library

Within every team there are channels. These channels are like a place where your entire team discusses a particular theme, like the ongoing project updates. Every channel has its file folder where you can share files for that precise channel. Before you can access this folder you will go to and select the **Files** tab above the conversation box.

In the library, you either upload an existing file or create a fresh one. When a file is uploaded, it creates another copy in teams.

Upload existing files

There are two major ways to upload existing files into your library. Both processes start by going to the files folder for your channel and both methods, by default, upload copies of your files to the channel file folder.

- **Drag and drop** - Using your mouse, drag the file from its current location and drop it on the Teams box among the files.

- **Upload** - Select **Upload**, then select the file you wish to upload and click **Open**.

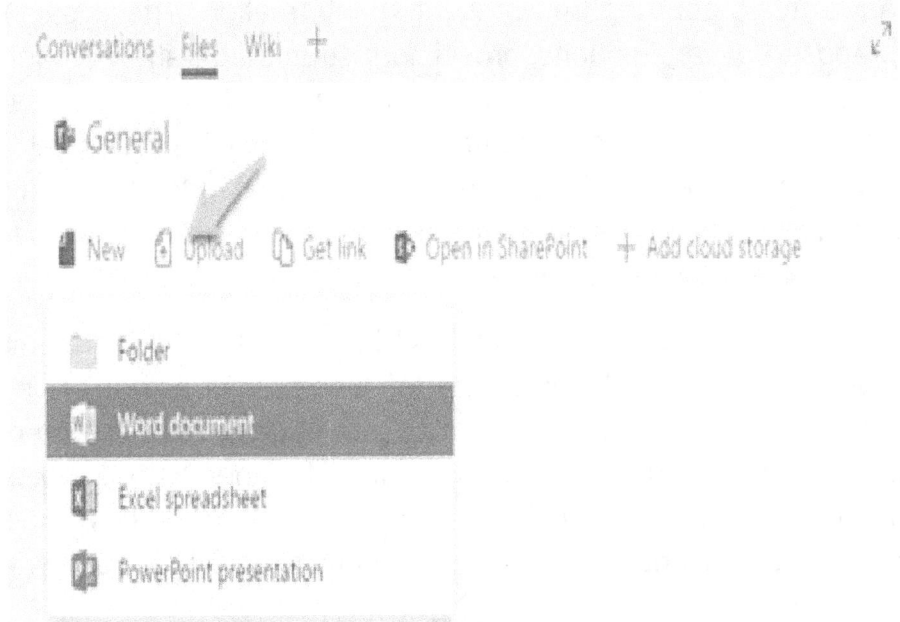

The file you uploaded can be reachable by all members of your team. Just as in SharePoint, you can pin exact files to the top of your list for easy contact.

THE WIKI TAB

CREATE A WIKI TAB

All channel comes with a **Wiki** tab.

To add a whole new **Wiki** tab, Choose to **Add a tab** + next to the other tab names in the channel. Choose **Wiki** from the tab gallery.

Write content for your Wiki tab

Within your Wiki tab, you'll discover a plethora of formatting options at your disposal, allowing you to customize your content precisely as you envision it. Whether you prefer bold statements for emphasis, italicized text for nuance, or underlined phrases for distinction, the Wiki tab offers a versatile array of tools to elevate your content. Each document within your Wiki tab is referred to as a "page," serving as a canvas for organizing and presenting information. These pages are composed of various units, providing a structured framework for your ideas and materials. To begin crafting your content, simply assign a name to your page and commence authoring its individual units. Whenever you wish to introduce a new segment, effortlessly navigate to the left side of the page and select the option to add a new section, facilitating seamless content expansion.

Navigating through your Wiki tab is a breeze, thanks to the intuitive table of subjects displayed on the left side of your screen. This table serves as a navigational aid, enabling swift traversal between pages and facilitating consolidation efforts. Whether you're exploring different topics or streamlining your content, the table of subjects empowers efficient navigation and organization within your Wiki tab environment.

Chat from Wiki tab

Start a chat in a unit

If you prefer not to add comments directly within a specific section, you can initiate a conversation within the tab itself by choosing "Section Conversation" located to the right of the relevant section. This allows you to post queries or leave notes without directly modifying the content of the section. Should there already be remarks within the tab's discussion, you'll be able to view them in the channel. Additionally, you'll be notified if someone has left notes in your Wiki tab, as "Section Conversation" will appear at the top of your page.

BROWSING AND ADDING APPS

ADD APP TO TEAMS

Add to team button can be used to install the application to a team. Bear it in your mind that this is only for apps that could be installed in a team scope. The Add to team button is not available for apps that could be installed in personal scope.

1. Search for the app you like, and then choose the app by left-clicking the app name.
2. Choose to **Add to the team**.
3. In the **Add to team** panel, the quest for a team you like to add the apps too, select the team, and then click **Apply**.

EXPLORING POPULAR APPS

Here are five things to know about Microsoft teams apps:

1. Apps in the tab can be used in chats and channels.

In Microsoft Teams, the versatility of applications extends seamlessly into your conversations and collaborative spaces. As you engage with various team members, each interaction brings forth unique insights and necessitates diverse tools. One powerful feature enabling this dynamic collaboration is the ability to integrate essential files and applications directly into your chats and channels as tabs.

Consider a scenario where your team frequently references a shared OneNote notebook throughout the day. To streamline your workflow within Teams and ensure quick access to this indispensable resource, you can easily incorporate it as a tab within any chat or channel. This straightforward process facilitates effortless navigation and instant retrieval of critical information, enhancing productivity and fostering effective communication. By adding tabs to your Teams environment, you empower yourself and your team members to seamlessly transition between conversations and relevant tools, eliminating the need for cumbersome navigation across multiple platforms. Whether it's accessing important documents, reviewing project milestones, or collaborating on shared tasks, the ability to customize tabs ensures that your workspace remains tailored to your specific requirements.

To initiate this integration, simply navigate to the desired chat or channel, click on the "+" icon at the top, and select the option to add a tab. From there, you can choose from a wide range of available applications and files, including OneNote, SharePoint, Planner, and more. This intuitive interface puts the power of customization directly in your hands, allowing you to optimize your Teams experience according to your workflow preferences.

2. Messages could be more than text.

Some applications allow you to insert content from the app right into Teams mails. These emails are chock full of information, have functions, or simply look nice. For you to use one, choose beneath the box where you type a message and choose an app.

Right-click a favorite app to **Pin** it for tranquil access.

3. **Some apps reply to questions and follow instructions.**

The benefit of a team in collaboration with teammates, a lesser-known advantage is working with bots. You can relate with bots by @mentioning them in conversations, channels, or search. For instants, you can chat with Planner to create a new poll exact from within a message. Bots might not give you similar warm, uncertain feelings as your coworkers, but they can save you time by handling definite responsibilities.

4. **App notifications informed the right people.**

Are there certain notifications that are valuable to the whole team? Go to the channel you like, select **More options > Connectors**, and select an app. Then you will be encouraged to organize notifications.

5. **Some apps bargain a personal view.**

Any app with an individual view will show on the left side of Teams. From this point, you can look at your responsibilities or you just have a place to do your own thing.

Right-click any app icon to **Pin** for easy contact.

POPULAR APPS FROM MICROSOFT

Microsoft Teams is a multifaceted application boasting an extensive array of features that span various functionalities. Its richness in capabilities often necessitates additional guidance to fully explore its potential. Moreover, the competence of Microsoft Teams can be further enhanced through the integration of numerous apps and extensions tailored to diverse needs. These supplementary tools not only facilitate seamless collaboration but also serve as invaluable aids for individuals across various professions and industries, enabling them to work with greater efficiency and efficacy.

GitHub

GitHub stands as one of the foremost developer platforms, serving as a cornerstone for collaborative coding endeavors worldwide. The GitHub app tailored for Teams emerges as a pivotal tool in facilitating seamless integration and real-time updates within your project ecosystem. Its intuitive interface ensures that staying abreast of the latest developments in your repositories becomes effortless and spontaneous.

This indispensable add-on empowers users to effortlessly peruse through a plethora of issues and pull requests directly from within the familiar confines of Microsoft Teams. By bridging the gap between these two platforms, it streamlines communication and enhances productivity, ultimately serving as a catalyst for efficient project management. Indeed, the GitHub app for Teams emerges as a primary time-saving solution for developers and teams alike, offering a seamless workflow and eliminating the need for constant context-switching between different tools.

Moreover, for those operating within more sensitive or private environments, GitHub offers an enterprise-grade solution. The GitHub Enterprise app caters specifically to individuals and organizations leveraging private repositories, ensuring robust security measures while still providing the same level of seamless integration and productivity-enhancing features. In conclusion, whether you're collaborating on open-source projects or working within a secure corporate environment, GitHub's suite of applications, including the GitHub app for Teams and GitHub Enterprise, stands as indispensable assets, fostering efficient collaboration and driving innovation in the realm of software development.

Polly

"Polly, integrated with Microsoft Teams, empowers you to effortlessly generate opinion polls within your team's communication channels, facilitating collective decision-making on a wide array of topics. Whether it's determining the course of action for a substantial project or pinpointing the optimal timing for a meeting, this user-friendly application fosters seamless collaboration and enables real-time feedback collection. With Polly, cooperative decision-making becomes not just efficient, but also spontaneous, enhancing productivity and team synergy within Microsoft Teams."

Google Analytics

If you're actively involved in web analytics as part of your professional duties, chances are you've encountered Google Analytics at some point. However, with the introduction of Google Analytics apps for Teams, your reporting experience takes a significant leap. Instead of navigating to your Google Analytics dashboard, you can now receive reports directly within the Microsoft Teams app. This seamless integration streamlines your workflow, ensuring quick access to vital insights without the need to switch between platforms.

Salesforce

The Salesforce application designed for Microsoft Teams offers a seamless integration, facilitating the dissemination of updates to any Teams channel it's assigned to. Whether you're keen on staying promptly informed about critical issues or ensuring that your team remains updated on all relevant developments within Salesforce, this application proves indispensable. Its functionality serves as a vital conduit, streamlining communication and ensuring that important information is effectively communicated across Teams channels, thereby enhancing collaboration and productivity within your organization.

Power BI

Power BI revolutionizes the way organizations interact with data, providing a seamless experience for inspecting reports and deliberating over insights gleaned from Microsoft's robust business analytics platform. For businesses leveraging Power BI, integrating it into their decision-making toolkit is a strategic imperative. By doing so, they streamline their processes, eliminating the need to toggle between multiple applications to analyze business intelligence and arrive at critical decisions. With Power BI seamlessly integrated into their workflows, teams can collaborate more effectively, harnessing the power of data to drive informed strategies and achieve organizational objectives with greater efficiency and precision.

App Studio

If you're looking to tailor Microsoft Teams apps to suit your specific requirements, installing Microsoft's App Studio is your first step. Once integrated into your Microsoft Teams environment, App Studio serves as your guide through the process of crafting Teams apps within a user-friendly, low-code environment. This approach is particularly beneficial for individuals who aren't developers but still seek to enhance the functionality of Teams according to their unique needs.

Health Hero

Implementing health initiatives like fitness contests through platforms like Microsoft Teams sounds like a fantastic idea to combat the potential rise in sedentary behavior post-pandemic. It's crucial to prioritize physical and mental well-being, especially when many are working remotely and may have less opportunity for physical activity. These kinds of initiatives can not only promote healthier habits but also foster a sense of community and camaraderie among colleagues. Plus, using technology to track progress and create friendly competition adds a fun element to staying healthy.

Microsoft Weekly Newsletter

Be your own company's Microsoft insider by reading these Windows and Office tips, tricks, and cheat sheets.

POPULAR APPS FROM THIRD-PARTY COMPANIES

Connectors

Connectors serve as invaluable bridges facilitating the seamless integration of third-party applications like Twitter, Skype, Dropbox, and many others into Microsoft Teams. They empower users to receive updates and notifications from their favorite services without having to navigate away from the Teams platform. For instance, software development teams can leverage Connectors to effortlessly incorporate GitHub, enabling them to efficiently track their projects, while marketing teams can utilize Subtleties to effectively manage their CRM activities without leaving the Teams environment. In simpler terms, a Connector acts as a wrapper for APIs, enabling Microsoft Teams to establish connections and exchange information with external applications. When updates or actions occur in other apps, Connectors generate cards containing concise summaries or action items, which are then shared in group feeds within Teams.

Connectors operate based on webhooks, a widely adopted method for establishing asynchronous communication with web applications. This approach offers a straightforward alternative to utilizing JavaScript-based callback functions. Presently, Microsoft Teams provides a standardized publish-and-subscribe mechanism, enabling users to easily subscribe to webhooks and receive timely updates within the platform.To avoid these aggravations, operators can merely get Connectors from within Teams and modify them as required. Although physically arranging a Connector can make it more supple and well fit to your needs, it is also more complex. Nevertheless, there is adequate online certification on how to integrate Connectors, and all you need is the URL of a suitable webhook.

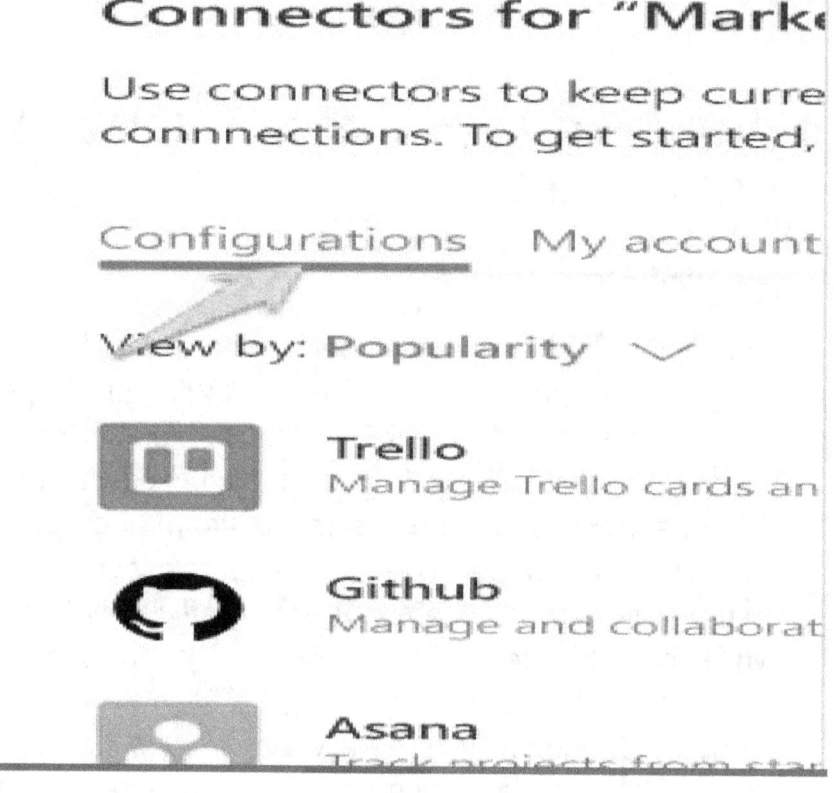

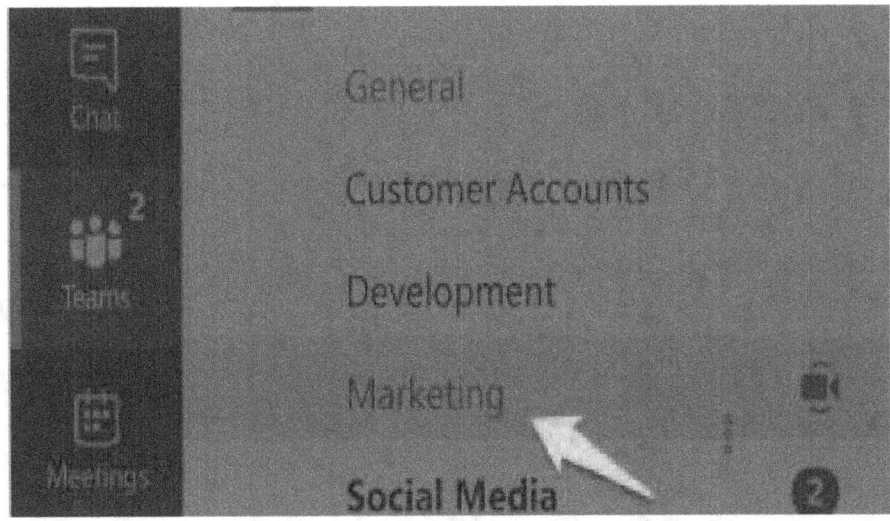

Bots

Embracing a more nuanced perspective, one might aptly characterize bots as sophisticated conversational engines. Their capacity to seamlessly interact with human operators, whether through organic dialogue or structured command-line interfaces, serves to enrich the collective understanding within Teams. To integrate any third-party bot into Teams, adherence to the Microsoft Bot Framework is imperative. This entails uploading the bot to the Microsoft Bot Directory, ensuring compatibility with the framework's architecture. Alternatively, auxiliary tools such as Howdy Botkit and Message.io offer avenues for adapting bots originally tailored for specific platforms, facilitating their utilization across diverse applications.

Within the expansive repository of the Microsoft Bot Directory, a plethora of pre-integrated bots awaits discovery. These bots, meticulously crafted by startups, corporate collaborators, and Microsoft's own engineering teams, embody diverse functionalities and cater to a spectrum of organizational needs. Since bots can be customized, they permit you to provide a comfortable and more collaborative experience to your operators. Bots can be automated to give a structured set of replies to operator mails, perform a specific role in your Team's conversation, and even help operators find what they are searching for.

IT admins have power over which bots are accessible to their end-users from the portal.

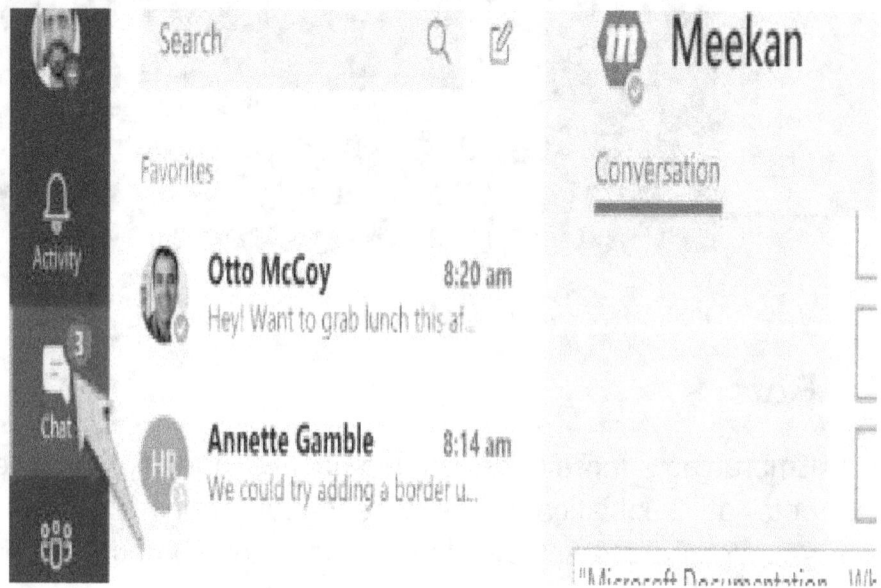

Tabs

Tabs in Microsoft Teams offer a seamless integration experience, allowing users to access complete third-party services directly within the Teams interface. This functionality is particularly valuable when you require more than just a fleeting glance at activity but need to effectively manage a significant amount of information. For example, if your support team needs to monitor remaining tickets or your sales team wants to review recent orders, tabs provide the perfect solution.

Technically, a tab is housed within a separate Microsoft Teams container known as an iframe, which is embedded within Teams itself. Integration at the tab level begins with creating a blueprint of the information that will be displayed within the tab, including a link to the configuration page. This configuration page empowers users to easily customize various settings such as icons, text, and other tab features to suit their specific needs.

Tabs serve as dedicated repositories for specific information and offer a dynamic window into third-party applications within the context of a team's channel. Users can seamlessly switch between tabs while continuing to communicate with their channel colleagues, fostering smoother collaboration and facilitating multitasking. This integration capability enhances productivity by keeping relevant information readily accessible within the Teams environment.

SETTING PERMISSIONS FOR APPS

App Permission Policies

"Implementation of app permission policies serves as a robust mechanism for exerting control over the selection of applications accessible to specific operators within your educational institution. Through these policies, you wield the power to authorize or restrict the usage of applications originating from Microsoft, third-party developers, as well as those developed internally within your institution.

These app permission policies offer a myriad of benefits, some of which include:

Tailoring Access for Custom Applications: One significant advantage lies in the ability to tailor access permissions for custom-built applications, ensuring that only designated operators with specific roles or responsibilities can utilize these bespoke tools. This granular control not only enhances security but also streamlines operational efficiency by aligning application access with organizational hierarchies and workflows.

Simplifying Operator Onboarding and Training: Particularly valuable during the deployment phase of platforms such as Teams across your institution, app permission policies play a pivotal role in simplifying the operator experience. By curating the selection of available applications based on relevance and utility, these policies mitigate the complexities associated with navigating a vast array of tools, thereby expediting the onboarding process for new users. This, in turn, facilitates smoother transitions and accelerates proficiency gains, ultimately fostering a more conducive environment for collaboration and productivity.

In essence, the judicious implementation of app permission policies empowers educational institutions to exercise precise control over their digital ecosystem, promoting security, efficiency, and seamlessness in the utilization of technology resources."

Create a custom app permission policy

If you which to control the apps that are present for dissimilar groups of operators in your organization, create and allocate one or more custom app permission policies. You can generate and allocate distinct custom policies depending on whether apps are issued by Microsoft, third parties, or your group. It is significant to know that after you generate a custom policy, you can not alter it if third-party apps are restricted in org-wide app settings.

1. In the left steering of the Microsoft Teams admin center, go to **Teams apps** > **Permission policies**.

2. Tick **Add**.

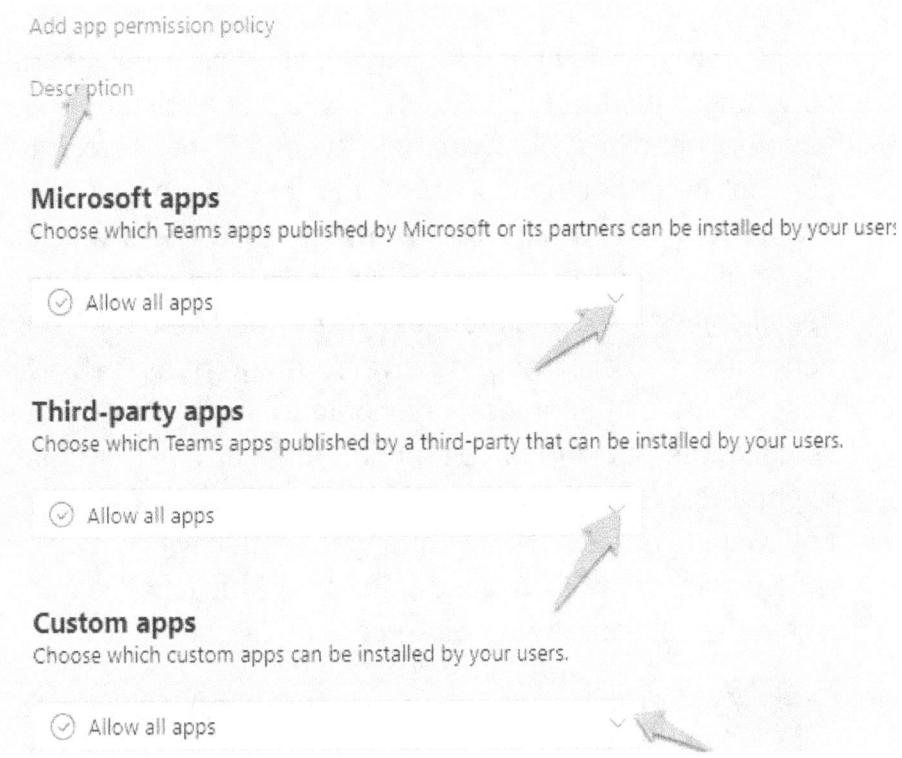

3. Enter a name and description for the policy.

4. Under **Microsoft apps**, **Third-party apps**, and **Custom apps**, select one of the following:

    - **Allow all apps**
    - **Allow specific apps and block all others**
    - **Block specific apps and allow all others**
    - **Block all apps**

5. If you selected **Allow all apps**, all the apps will be allow

6. Click **Save**.

GETTING CHATTY WITH BOTS

Microsoft Teams bots

"Designed with the aim of simplifying our daily routines and supporting us in our everyday tasks, a bot is a digital assistant that streamlines various aspects of our lives. In the context of Microsoft Teams, this concept is further enhanced by the integration of the Microsoft Bot Framework. This framework provides developers with the tools and capabilities needed to create their own customized bots tailored to specific needs and preferences. Within the Microsoft Teams platform, accessing and exploring the diverse range of available bots is made easy. Users can effortlessly navigate to the 'More Options' menu and select 'More apps' to unveil a comprehensive list of bots ready to be integrated into their Teams experience. This seamless integration of bots within Teams not only enhances productivity but also offers users a convenient way to access additional functionalities and resources within the collaborative environment of Teams."

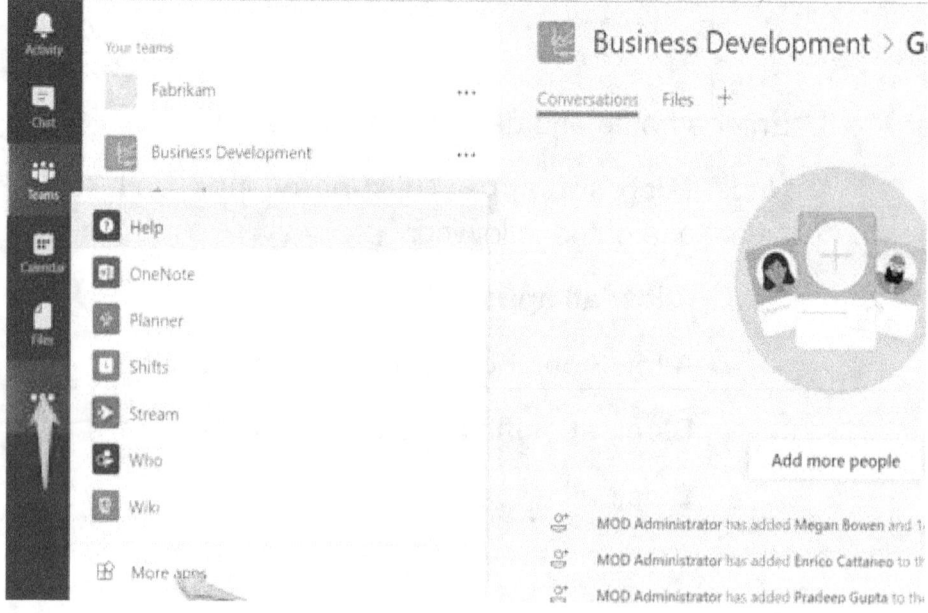

After clicking on **More apps**, an overview of all available bots appears:

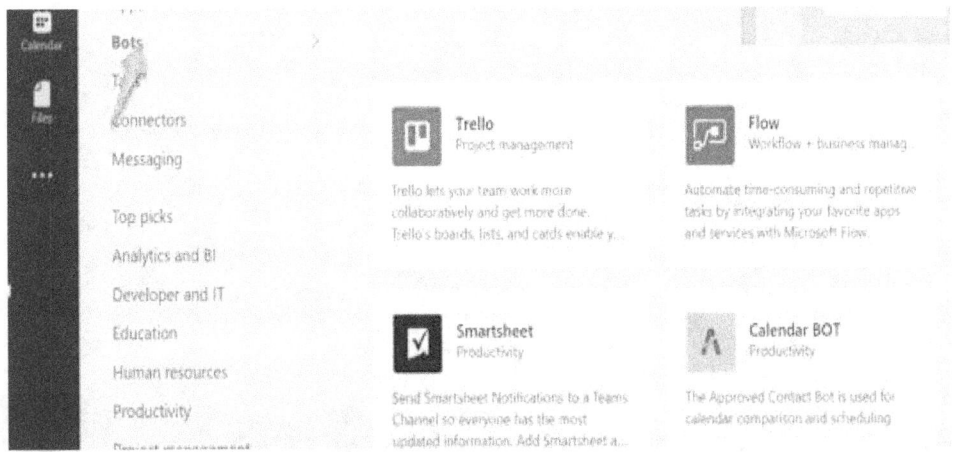

The collection of bots you can select from has developed significantly since the unveiling of Teams. It wouldn't be explained in detail because there are different types of I won't go into too much detail about all the different kinds simply because there are so many—but I would counsel you to find a bot that fits your current needs and test run it.

Microsoft comprises its bot—a personal subordinate app called Who. Powered by the Microsoft Graph, Which lets you search for individuals in your group by name or theme.

You can inquire from its diversity of questions by typing in the start of simple phrases:

For example, you can easily find the manager of one of your coworkers:

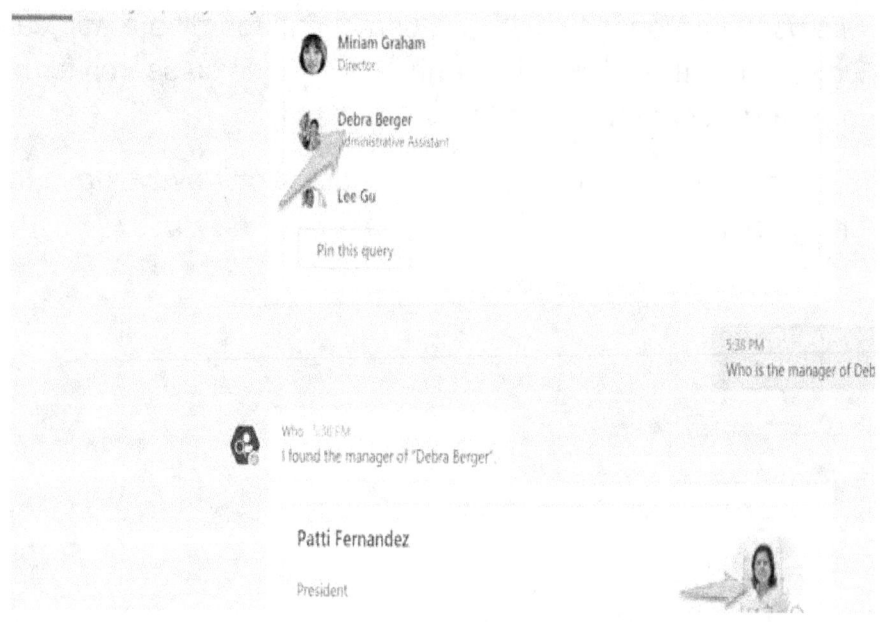

Who Bot can also provide a dynamic organization chart:

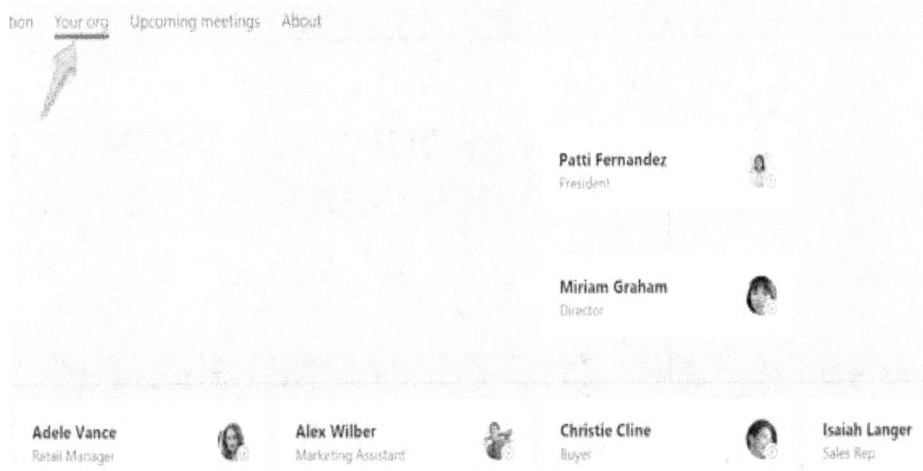

Or a list of your upcoming meetings:

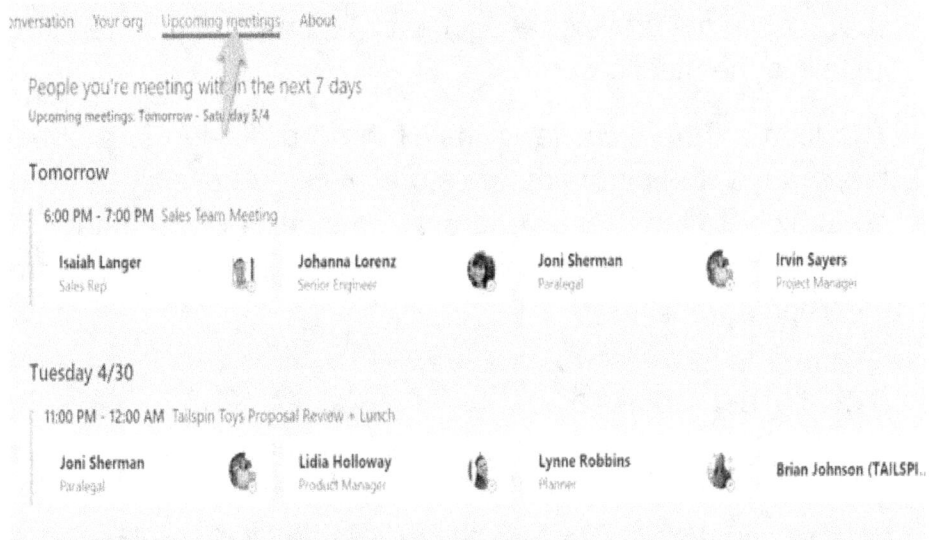

Who has huge potential when it comes to connecting and finding people?

CHAPTER 6

UNSHACKLING YOURSELF WITH TEAMS ON MOBILE

INSTALLING THE TEAMS MOBILE APPS

Teams could be installed on a mobile device in dissimilar ways. The simplest way is to open the Google Play Store or the Apple App Store and search for the Teams mobile app. An alternative way is to use your mobile net browser and log into **Teams** and then tap the icon for installing the mobile app.

The icon on the website to install the mobile app is a shortcut that takes you to the pertinent app store. You will possibly find it easier to go straight to the iOS or Android app store and search for Microsoft Teams instead of trying to circumnavigate your mobile net browser to the Teams website.

Installing on iOS

To install the Teams mobile app on your iPhone or iPad:

1. **Open the Apple App Store on your iOS device.**
2. **Then tap the Search icon in the store and type** Microsoft Teams. You ensure that you select the Microsoft app, as shown.
3. **Tap the download link to install the app on your device.**
4. **Once you finish downloading and installing the app, tap the Open button.**

Installing the Teams app from the Apple App Store.

Installing on Android

To install the Teams mobile app on your Android phone or tablet:

1. **Open the Google Play Store on your Android device.**

2. **Tap the Search icon in the store and type** Microsoft Teams. You make sure you select the Microsoft app, as shown.

3. **Tap the Install button to install the app on your device.**

4. **Once you finish downloading and installing, tap the Open button.**

Installing the Teams app from the Google Play Store.

When you launch the Teams mobile application, you'll encounter a login screen prompting you to sign in. Here, you have the option to tap the "Sign In" button, initiating the process. Following this, you'll be prompted to enter your Office 365 credentials, which you would have set up during the Office 365 trial registration.

Upon successful login, Teams will load and provide you with a series of instructions to familiarize yourself with the app's functionality. Once you've completed this initial guidance, you'll be ready to begin utilizing Teams for your tasks and collaborations, as we'll explore further in the next section. If you've previously signed in with any other Office 365 application on your mobile device, such as Outlook, you have the convenience of selecting that account. Teams will then seamlessly log you in using the credentials already stored securely on your device, streamlining the login process for your convenience.If I prefer to avoid signing up for Office 365, I can also sign up for a free account by downloading the app on your mobile device and tapping the Sign Up for Free button as shown below.

Signing in to the Teams mobile app.

Find your way around the Teams mobile app

What truly impresses me about Teams is its seamless compatibility across various devices. Whether I'm using the desktop version on my laptop, the mobile app on my phone, or even switching between different platforms like Mac, iPad, Android phone, Windows laptop, and iPhone, the experience remains consistent. Microsoft's approach with Teams, being a relatively new application developed just a few years ago, was to design all its clients simultaneously. As a result, regardless of the device you're on, the core functionalities and features remain consistent. While there may be slight variations in the interfaces to optimize them for specific devices, once you grasp the basic concepts of Teams, navigating through any client feels intuitive and comfortable.

We have discussed previously, we talk about the left navigation pane in the Teams web and desktop and laptop apps. The mobile Teams app is alike except instead of retrieving the Teams icons in the left navigation pane, the app embraces tabs across the bottom of the screen, as shown below.

To access your profile settings, navigate to the Settings icon on your screen. This icon is often referred to as the "hamburger menu" due to its three-layered appearance resembling a hamburger. Once you tap on this icon, a menu will appear where you can adjust various aspects of your profile. Within the profile settings, you have the option to set your status and status message, allowing you to communicate your availability or mood to others. Additionally, you can toggle notifications on or off according to your preferences, ensuring you receive important updates or remain undisturbed when necessary.

Furthermore, this menu provides information about any new features or updates to the application, keeping you informed about the latest developments. Additionally, you can access a range of additional settings tailored specifically for the mobile app, allowing you to customize your experience further to suit your needs.

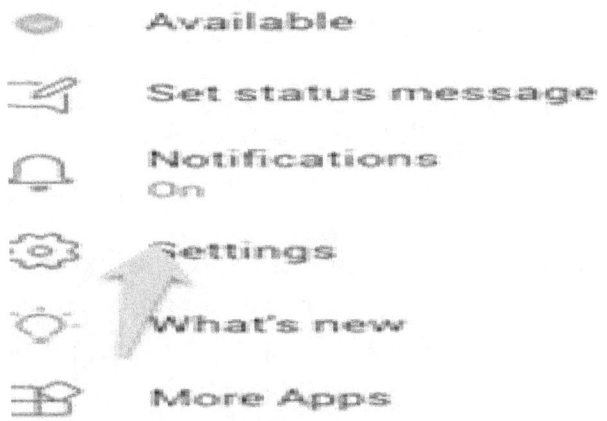

Tapping your way through Teams

The Teams mobile application, much like its counterparts, is meticulously crafted for interaction through tactile screen manipulation on your smartphone or tablet. Our experience has shown that navigating Teams via touch is intuitive; however, the transition from traditional keyboard and mouse inputs to finger-based interaction entails minimal adjustments..

Interacting with messages

Using reactions, you can add a sad face, a thumbs up, or any number of dissimilar emojis to your conversation messages. Besides, you can interrelate with messages in different ways. You can

- Save a message so that you can rapidly find and analyst it later.
- Unread a message so that it continues to show as new in Teams.
- Copy a connection to the straight message.

- Open the mail in the immersive reader, which will help in reading the message for you and show you every word as it is read.

- Turn on notifications for the message thread.

- Generate a new poll that will be involved in the message.

If you are reacting to your message, then you have additional alternatives such as being able to edit or delete the note. If you don't view these alternatives for your mails, then your manager has turned off your capability to edit or delete messages.

When using Teams with your keyboard and mouse, you can soar your mouse over a message or click the elision to view these communications, as shown.

Reacting to a message using Teams on a desktop or laptop computer.

Nevertheless, when you are using Teams on your mobile device, soaring your finger isn't a choice. Instead, you need to tap and hold on to the message to bring up a similar menu, as shown.

If you are trapped and cannot find a menu when steering Teams on a mobile device, try tapping and holding as an option. Using a mouse, you can soar your mouse over essentials of the boundary to view menus, but soaring is not an option when you are using fingers.

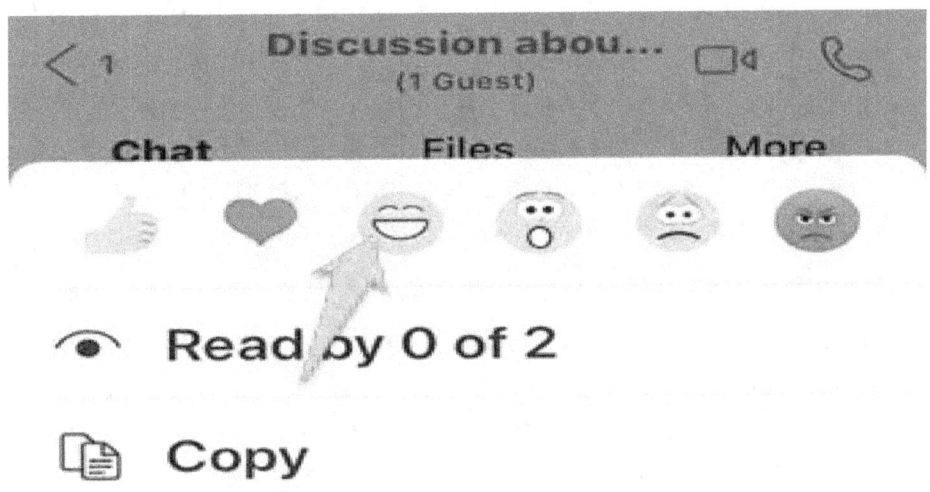

Reacting to a message using Teams on a phone or tablet.

If you are reacting to a message in a chat, you must tap and hold to access the reaction options, but if you are reacting to a message thread in a channel, you will see a tiny ellipsis and you can tap that, too. I find it easier to just tap and hold a message in either a chat or a channel to bring up the menu shown in the figure.

GETTING USED TO NAVIGATION

As stated earlier in this chapter, steering through the Teams mobile app is faintly dissimilar to when you use a keyboard and mouse. Relatively than clicking navigational icons laterally on the left side of the app, in the mobile version these icons are found laterally at the bottom of the app.

The knowledge is improved for mobile devices, which means the flow is faintly dissimilar in the mobile app because the volume of space on a mobile device is lesser than laptop or desktop computer screen. The major key dissimilarity in navigation is that the screens you steer may need more taps to the screen than the related clicks with your mouse.

Steering into your conversations on your mobile device is much related to keyboard performance. Nevertheless, if you tap the Teams option, you will be offered all the teams and channels you have. You need to tap again to open one of those channels, as shown in the following figure. On a big monitor, you can view all the teams and channels at a time you view the related emails in the channel. For a mobile app, you need to make another tap in direction to get into the channel, and if you need to change channels, you need to tap the back icon and then choose a dissimilar channel.

Steering Teams on a mobile device can take more taps than the related clicks when using Teams on a laptop or desktop. Even if the mobile app takes more work to navigate, it's worth the energy because the know-how on a mobile device is designed for lesser screens and using your fingers in place of a mouse.

	Teams	
PI	Portal Integrators...	...
	General	>
	Morale Events	>
MP	My Private Team	...
	General	>
MF	My First Team	...
	General	>

Tapping a channel in the list of teams on a mobile phone.

Steps to Tap a Channel in Microsoft Teams on a Mobile Phone

Open the Microsoft Teams App: Launch the Microsoft Teams application on your mobile phone.

1. Access the Teams Section: On the bottom menu, tap on the "Teams" icon. This will show a list of all the teams you are part of.

2. Select a Team: Scroll through the list to find the team you want to access. Tap on the name of the team to open it.

3. View Channels: Once you have opened the team, you will see a list of channels under the team name. Channels are sub-sections within a team where specific topics or projects are discussed.

4. Tap on a Channel: Scroll through the channels to find the one you need. Tap on the channel name to open it. This will take you to the conversation and files specific to that channel.

Summary

By following these steps, you can easily navigate through your teams and channels in Microsoft Teams on your mobile phone. The pictorial illustrations provide a visual guide to help you understand the process better.

CONCLUSION

In conclusion, harnessing the capabilities of Microsoft Teams emerges as pivotal in fostering seamless and effective communication within teams. Delving into the intricacies of the slides reveals a multifaceted approach towards optimizing team management and tailoring settings to cater to specific requirements. This comprehensive presentation serves as a beacon, illuminating the path towards mastering the utilization of emojis, GIFs, and stickers within the Microsoft Teams ecosystem, thereby infusing conversations with vibrancy and expression. Moreover, it transcends mere functionality by exploring a rich tapestry of supplementary applications designed to augment collaborative endeavors within teams, thereby fostering innovation and productivity.

Furthermore, the presentation serves as a compendium of knowledge, addressing the quintessential query of how to navigate the labyrinthine process of downloading and installing Teams across an array of devices. Whether it be the familiar confines of a laptop, the steadfast reliability of a desktop, or the ubiquitous presence of mobile devices, the elucidation provided offers clarity and guidance, ensuring seamless integration into the Teams environment. This exhaustive exploration not only demystifies the installation process but also empowers users with the confidence to traverse the digital landscape with ease and proficiency. Thus, the presentation stands not only as a solution to immediate queries but also as a springboard towards comprehensive mastery of the Microsoft Teams platform.

www.ingramcontent.com/pod-product-compliance
Lightning Source LLC
Chambersburg PA
CBHW082213220526
45470CB00010B/3148